THE COMMUNIST MANIFESTO

❧

PRINCIPLES OF COMMUNISM

❧

THE
COMMUNIST MANIFESTO
150 YEARS LATER

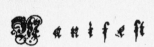

Manifest

der

Kommunistischen Partei.

Veröffentlicht im Februar 1848.

Proletarier aller Länder vereinigt Euch!

London.
Gedruckt in der Office der „Bildungs-Gesellschaft für Arbeiter"
von J. E. Burghard.
46, LIVERPOOL STREET, BISHOPSGATE.

Cover of the first edition of the *Communist Manifesto*,
published anonymously, in German, in 1848

THE COMMUNIST MANIFESTO

Karl Marx
and Friedrich Engels

PRINCIPLES OF COMMUNISM

Friedrich Engels
Translation by Paul M. Sweezy

THE
COMMUNIST MANIFESTO
150 YEARS LATER

Ellen Meiksins Wood

Monthly Review Press
New York

"Editor's Preface" by Christopher Phelps, "Foreword" by Paul M. Sweezy, and
"The Communist Manifesto 150 Years Later" by Ellen Meiksins Wood © 1998
by Monthly Review Press
"Principles of Communism" by Friedrich Engels, translation by Paul M. Sweezy
© 1964 by Monthly Review Press

Library of Congress Cataloging-in-Publication Data

Marx, Karl, 1818-1883.
      The Communist manifesto / Karl Marx and Friedrich Engels.
   Principles of communism / Friedrich Engels. The Communist manifesto
   one hundred and fifty years later / Ellen Meiksins Wood.
            p.   cm.
      ISBN 0-85345-936-3 (pbk.)
      1. Communism. I. Engels, Friedrich, 1820-1895. II. Engels, Friedrich,
   1820-1895. Principles of communism.   III. Wood, Ellen Meiksins.
   Communist manifesto one hundred and fifty years later. IV. Title.
   HX39.5.A5122 1998
   335.4'22—dc21   98-9538
                                                       CIP

Monthly Review Press
122 West 27th Street
New York, NY 10001

Manufactured in Canada

10 9 8 7 6 5 4

CONTENTS

EDITOR'S PREFACE

By general reckoning, the *Communist Manifesto*, first published as an anonymous German-language pamphlet in London in 1848, ranks just below the Bible and Koran on the list of all-time bestsellers. Given that commanding stature, it is remarkable that so many editions of the *Manifesto* are preceded by long introductions—anti-introductions, to be precise—which aim to discredit the work rather than illuminate it, to disabuse and discourage readers rather than inform or instruct them.

This edition is of a different persuasion. Highly respectful of the historical materialist method and socialist commitment of Karl Marx and Friedrich Engels, it at the same time eschews hagiography or endorsement of any particular points in the document which have not withstood the test of experience.

A new foreword by Paul M. Sweezy, longtime co-editor of *Monthly Review* magazine and author of many important works of Marxist theory, takes stock of the enduring pertinence of the *Manifesto*, despite the unanticipated twists of subsequent history.

The *Manifesto* itself features a distinguished typeface. Set by hand in 1933 for a limited edition of five hundred copies, it is, as we are sure readers will agree, a pleasure to read. The text follows the standard 1888 English translation approved by Engels.

The *Manifesto* is followed by an important supplementary document: Engels' first draft of the *Manifesto*, written in 1847 in question-

and-answer form, and later published under the title *Principles of Communism* (translation by Paul M. Sweezy, first published by Monthly Review Press in 1952).

A concluding essay by Ellen Meiksins Wood, "The *Communist Manifesto* 150 Years Later," rounds out the volume. Co-editor of *Monthly Review* and author of *The Retreat from Class* (1986), among other important contributions to social and political theory, Wood subjects the ideas and enduring relevance of the *Manifesto* to precise analysis. In marked contrast to the anti-introductions favored by many commercial publishers, Wood writes in basic appreciation of the method of Marx and Engels. Her sympathetic yet critical perspective is sure to be helpful to a new generation of students and general readers striving to make sense of the significance and merit of Marxism.

CHRISTOPHER PHELPS

EDITORIAL DIRECTOR,
MONTHLY REVIEW PRESS
FEBRUARY 1998

FOREWORD

This new edition of the *Communist Manifesto* marks the 150th anniversary of the publication of that landmark document, by far the most famous expression of the ideas and aims of the revolutionary movement that was born in Western Europe in the seventeenth and eighteenth centuries and has since grown to global dimensions, along with the capitalist system which it reflects and which provides the reason for its existence.

As it happens, the publication of this new edition of the *Manifesto* coincides with the unfolding of the latest of capitalism's recurring economic crises which are so strikingly described by the authors as one of the system's quintessential features. Despite the continuing efforts of bourgeois economists to understand this phenomenon, let alone to devise a cure for it, "these crises by their periodical return put on its trial, each time more threateningly, the entire bourgeois society. . . . There breaks out an epidemic that in all earlier epochs would have seemed an absurdity, the epidemic of overproduction." This is precisely the epidemic that is now spreading over the entire global economy.

While periodic economic crises were judged by Marx and Engels to be a permanent and growing threat to capitalism, they were not considered to be the cause of its eventual overthrow and replacement by a more rational and egalitarian society. That role was reserved for class struggle culminating in a proletarian revolution. And on this subject they were heavily influenced by the time in which they were writing. Revolutions were the order of the day in 1848, and the authors of the *Manifesto* believed that Germany was "on the eve of a bourgeois revolution that is bound to be carried out under more advanced conditions of European civilization than existed in England in the seventeenth and in France in the eighteenth century," and that "the bourgeois revolution in Germany would be but the prelude to an immediately following proletarian revolution."

In reality, of course, history took a sharp turn soon after this was written, and capitalism entered one of its most expansive phases, lasting until the outbreak of the First World War in 1914. From then to the end of the twentieth century, class struggles, intermixed with national wars, raged with only occasional, and even then never completely peaceful, interludes. History's two greatest revolutions occurred in this century now drawing to a close, the first in Russia, the second in China. For a time it seemed that the world was destined to be divided into two antagonistic systems, one capitalist and the other seeking to realize a viable alternative. The result was the Cold War which dominated the second half of the century and ended with a clear-cut victory for capitalism.

The end of that phase came about ten years ago, almost too short even to register on history's clock, but long enough to demonstrate that capitalism's triumph was distinctly of the Pyrrhic variety. Bourgeois ideologists, dizzy with success, hastened to predict a new era of peace and prosperity stretching out into the indefinite future. If events had conformed to this vision, the hundred-and-fiftieth anniversary of the *Communist Manifesto* would probably have passed with hardly more than a brief obituary. But now with capitalism wallowing in a new multidimensional crisis—most visibly economic but also ideological, moral, and spiritual—the *Manifesto* assumes a new meaning and relevance.

Class struggles are not much in the news these days; capitalism's predominance, stemming from its victory in the Cold War, is still largely intact. But opposition from below is far from dead, and history suggests that it will grow, take on new forms, develop new strategies, and gradually recover the strength and determination to challenge a status quo that day by day becomes increasingly intolerable for all but a tiny minority of humankind.

PAUL M. SWEEZY

THE COMMUNIST MANIFESTO

Karl Marx
and Friedrich Engels

A spectre is haunting Europe, the spectre of Communism. All the powers of old Europe have entered into a holy alliance to exorcise this spectre; Pope and Czar, Metternich and Guizot, French Radicals and German police-spies.

Where is the party in opposition that has not been decried as communistic by its opponents in power? Where is the Opposition that has not hurled back the branding reproach of Communism, against the more advanced opposition parties, as well as against its reactionary adversaries?

Two things result from this fact:

1. Communism is already acknowledged by all European powers to be itself a power.

2. It is high time that Communists should openly, in the face of the whole world, publish their views, their aims, their tendencies, and meet this nursery tale of the spectre of Communism with a manifesto of the party itself.

To this end, Communists of various nationalities have assembled in London, and sketched the following manifesto, to be published in the English, French, German, Italian, Flemish, and Danish languages.

The history of all hitherto existing society is the history of class struggles.

Freeman and slave, patrician and plebeian, lord and serf, guild-master and journeyman, in a word, oppressor and oppressed, stood in constant opposition to one another, carried on an uninterrupted, now hidden, now open fight, a fight that each time ended either in a revolutionary reconstitution of society at large, or in the common ruin of the contending classes.

In the earlier epochs of history, we find almost every where a complicated arrangement of society into various orders, a manifold gradation of social rank. In ancient Rome we have patricians, knights, plebeians, slaves; in the Middle Ages, feudal lords, vassals, guild-masters, journeymen, apprentices, serfs; in almost all of these classes, again, subordinate gradations.

The modern bourgeois society that has sprouted from the ruins of feudal society has not done away with class antagonisms. It has but established new classes, new conditions of oppression, new forms of struggle in place of the old ones.

Our epoch, the epoch of the bourgeoisie, possesses, however, this distinctive feature; it has simplified the class antagonisms. Society as a whole is more and more splitting up into two great hostile camps, into two great classes directly facing each other: Bourgeoisie and Proletariat.

From the serfs of the Middle Ages sprang the chartered burghers of the earliest towns. From these burgesses the first elements of the bourgeoisie were developed.

The discovery of America, the rounding of the Cape, opened up fresh ground for the rising bourgeoisie. The East-Indian and Chinese markets, the colonization of America, trade with the colonies, the increase in the means of exchange and in commodities generally, gave to commerce, to navigation, to industry, an impulse never before known, and thereby, to the revolutionary element in the tottering feudal society, a rapid development.

The feudal system of industry, in which industrial production was monopolized by closed guilds, now no longer sufficed for the growing wants of the new markets. The manufacturing system took its place. The guild-masters were pushed on one side by the manufacturing middle-class; division of labor between the different corporate guilds vanished in the face of division of labor in each single workshop.

Meantime the markets kept ever growing, the demand, ever rising. Even manufacture no longer sufficed. Thereupon steam and machinery revolutionized industrial production. The place of manufacture was now taken by the giant, modern industry, the place of the industrial middle-class, by industrial millionaires, the leaders of whole industrial armies, the modern bourgeois.

Modern industry has established the world-market, for which the discovery of America paved the way. This market has given an immense development to commerce, to navigation, to communication by land. This development has, in its turn, reacted on the extension of industry; and in proportion as industry, commerce, navigation, railways extended, in the same proportion the bourgeoisie developed, increased its capital, and pushed into the background every class handed down from the Middle Ages.

We see, therefore, how the modern bourgeoisie is itself the product of a long course of development, of a series of revolutions in the modes of production and of exchange.

Each step in the development of the bourgeoisie

was accompanied by a corresponding political advance of that class. An oppressed class under the sway of the feudal nobility, it became an armed and self-governing association in the mediaeval commune; here independent urban republic (as in Italy and Germany), there taxable «third estate» of the monarchy (as in France); afterwards, in the period of manufacture proper, serving either the semi-feudal or the absolute monarchy as a counterpoise against the nobility, and, in fact, cornerstone of the great monarchies in general, the bourgeoisie has at last, since the establishment of Modern Industry and of the world-market, conquered for itself, in the modern representative State, exclusive political sway. The executive of the modern State is but a committee for managing the common affairs of the whole bourgeoisie.

The bourgeoisie has played a most revolutionary role in history.

The bourgeoisie, wherever it has got the upper hand, has put an end to all feudal, patriarchal, idyllic relations. It has pitilessly torn asunder the motley feudal ties that bound man to his «natural superiors», and has left remaining no other bond between man and man than naked self-interest, than callous «cash payment ». It has drowned the most heavenly ecstacies of religious fervor, of chivalrous enthusiasm, of philistine sentimentalism, in the icy water of egotistical calculation. It has resolved personal worth into exchange value, and in place of the numberless indefeasible chartered freedoms, has set up that single, unconscionable freedom, Free Trade. In one word, for exploitation, veiled by religious and political illusions, it has substituted naked, shameless, direct, brutal exploitation.

The bourgeoisie has stripped of its halo every occupation hitherto honored and looked up to with reverent awe. It has converted the physician, the lawyer, the priest, the poet, the man of science, into its paid wage-laborers.

The bourgeoisie has torn away from the family its sentimental veil, and has reduced the family relation to a mere money relation.

The bourgeoisie has disclosed how it came to pass that the brutal display of vigor in the Middle Ages, which Reactionists so much admire, found its fitting complement in the most slothful indolence. It has been the first to show what man's activity can bring about. It has accomplished wonders far surpassing Egyptian pyramids, Roman aqueducts, and Gothic cathedrals; it has conducted expeditions that put in the shade all former migrations of nations and crusades.

The bourgeoisie cannot exist without constantly revolutionizing the instruments of production, and thereby the relations of production, and with them the whole relations of society. Conservation of the old modes of production in unaltered form was, on the contrary, the first condition of existence for all earlier industrial classes. Constant revolutionizing of production, uninterrupted disturbance of all social conditions, everlasting uncertainty and agitation distinguish the bourgeois epoch from all earlier ones. All fixed, fast-frozen relations, with their train of ancient and venerable prejudices and opinions, are swept away, all new-formed ones become antiquated before they can ossify. All that is solid melts into air, all that is holy is profaned, and man is at last compelled to face with sober senses his real conditions of life, and his relations with his kind.

The need of a constantly expanding market for its products chases the bourgeoisie over the whole surface of the globe. It must nestle everywhere, settle everywhere, establish connections everywhere.

The bourgeoisie has through its exploitation of the

world-market given a cosmopolitan character to production and consumption in every country. To the great chagrin of Reactionists, it has drawn from under the feet of industry the national ground on which it stood. All old-established national industries have been destroyed or are daily being destroyed. They are dislodged by new industries, whose introduction becomes a life and death question for all civilized nations, by industries that no longer work up indigenous raw material, but raw material drawn from the remotest zones; industries whose products are consumed, not only at home, but in every quarter of the globe. In place of the old wants, satisfied by the production of the country, we find new wants, requiring for their satisfaction the products of distant lands and climes. In place of the old local and national seclusion and self-sufficiency, we have intercourse in every direction, universal interdependence of nations. And as in material, so also in intellectual production. The intellectual creations of individual nations become common property. National one-sidedness and narrow-mindedness become more and more impossible, and from the numerous national and local literatures there arises a world literature.

The bourgeoisie, by the rapid improvement of all instruments of production, by the immensely facilitated means of communication, draws all, even the most barbarian, nations into civilization. The cheap prices of its commodities are the heavy artillery with which it batters down all Chinese walls, with which it forces the barbarians' intensely obstinate hatred of foreigners to capitulate. It compels all nations, on pain of extinction, to adopt the bourgeois mode of production; it compels them to introduce what it calls civilization into their midst, i. e., to become bourgeois themselves. In a word, it creates a world after its own image.

The bourgeoisie has subjected the country to the rule of the towns. It has created enormous cities, has greatly increased the urban population as compared with the rural, and has thus rescued a considerable part of the population from the idiocy of rural life. Just as it has made the country dependent on the towns, so it has made barbarian and semi-barbarian countries dependent on the civilized ones, nations of peasants on nations of bourgeois, the East on the West.

The bourgeoisie keeps more and more doing away with the scattered state of the population, of the means of production, and of property. It has agglomerated population, centralized means of production, and has concentrated property in a few hands. The necessary consequence of this was political centralization. Independent, or but loosely connected provinces, with separate interests, laws, systems of taxation, and governments, became lumped together in one nation, with one government, one code of laws, one national class-interest, one frontier, and one customs tariff.

The bourgeoisie, during its rule of scarce one hundred years, has created more massive and more colossal productive forces than have all preceding generations together. Subjection of Nature's forces to man, machinery, application of chemistry to industry and agriculture, steam-navigation, railways, electric telegraphs, clearing of whole continents for cultivation, canalization of rivers, whole populations conjured out of the ground. What earlier century had even a presentiment that such productive forces slumbered in the lap of social labor?

We see then: the means of production and of exchange on whose foundation the bourgeoisie built itself up were generated in feudal society. At a certain stage in the development of these means of production and of exchange, the conditions under which feudal society produced and exchanged, the feudal organization of agriculture and manufacturing industry, in one word, the feudal relations of property became no longer compatible with the already developed productive forces; they became so many fetters. They had to burst asunder; they were burst asunder.

Into their places stepped free competition, accompanied by a social and political constitution adapted to it, and by the economical and political sway of the bourgeois class.

A similar movement is going on before our own eyes. Modern bourgeois society with its relations of production, of exchange and of property, a society that has conjured up such gigantic means of production and of exchange, is like the sorcerer, who is no longer able to control the powers of the nether world whom he has called up by his spells. For many a decade past the history of industry and commerce is but the history of the revolt of modern productive forces against modern conditions of production, against the property relations that are the conditions for the existence of the bourgeoisie and of its rule. It is enough to mention the commercial crises that by their periodical return put on its trial, each time more threateningly, the existence of the entire bourgeois society. In these crises a great part not only of the existing products but also of the previously created productive forces are periodically destroyed. In these crises there breaks out an epidemic that, in all earlier epochs, would have seemed an absurdity, the epidemic of overproduction. Society suddenly finds itself put back into a state of momentary barbarism; it appears as if a famine, a universal war of devastation had cut off the supply of every means of subsistence; industry and commerce seem to be destroyed; and why? Because there is too much civilization, too much means of subsistence, too much industry, too much commerce. The productive forces at the disposal of society no longer tend to further the development of the conditions of bourgeois property; on the contrary, they have become too powerful for these conditions, by which they are fettered, and so soon as they overcome these fetters, they bring disorder into the whole of bourgeois society, endanger the existence of bourgeois property. The conditions of bourgeois society are too narrow to comprise the wealth created by them. And how does the bourgeoisie get over these crises?

On the one hand by enforced destruction of a mass of productive forces; on the other, by the conquest of new markets, and by the more thorough exploitation of the old ones. That is to say, by paving the way for more extensive and more destructive crises, and by diminishing the means whereby crises are prevented.

The weapons with which the bourgeoisie felled feudalism to the ground are now turned against the bourgeoisie itself.

But not only has the bourgeoisie forged the weapons that bring death to itself; it has also called into existence the men who are to wield those weapons, the modern working-class, the proletarians.

In proportion as the bourgeoisie, i. e., capital, is developed, in the same proportion is the proletariat, the modern working-class, developed, a class of laborers, who live only so long as they find work, and who find work only so long as their labor increases capital. These laborers, who must sell themselves piecemeal, are a commodity, like every other article of commerce, and are consequently exposed to all the vicissitudes of competition, to all the fluctuations of the market.

Owing to the extensive use of machinery and to

division of labor, the work of the proletarians has lost all individual character, and, consequently, all charm for the workman. He becomes an appendage of the machine, and it is only the most simple, most monotonous, and most easily acquired knack that is required of him. Hence, the cost of production of a workman is restricted, almost entirely, to the means of subsistence that he requires for his maintenance, and for the propagation of his race. But the price of a commodity, and also of labor, is equal to its cost of production. In proportion, therefore, as the repulsiveness of the work increases, the wage decreases. Nay more, in proportion as the use of machinery and division of labor increases, in the same proportion the burden of toil also increases, whether by prolongation of the working hours, by increase of the work enacted in a given time, or by increased speed of the machinery, etc.

Modern industry has converted the little workshop of the patriarchal master into the great factory of the industrial capitalist. Masses of laborers, crowded into the factory, are organized like soldiers. As privates of the industrial army they are placed under the command of a perfect hierarchy of officers and sergeants. Not only are they the slaves of the bourgeois class, and of the bourgeois State, they are daily and hourly enslaved by the machine, by the overlooker, and, above all, by the individual bourgeois manufacturer himself. The more openly this despotism proclaims gain to be its end and aim, the more petty, the more hateful and the more embittering it is.

The less the skill and exertion or strength implied in manual labor, in other words, the more modern industry becomes developed, the more is the labor of men superseded by that of women. Differences of age and sex have no longer any distinctive social validity for the working class. All are instruments of labor, more or less expensive to use, according to their age and sex.

No sooner is the exploitation of the laborer by the manufacturer, so far at an end, that he receives his wages in cash, than he is set upon by the other portions of the bourgeoisie, the landlord, the shopkeeper, the pawnbroker, etc.

The lower strata of the Middle class, the small tradespeople, shopkeepers, and retired tradesmen generally, the handicraftsmen and peasants, all these sink gradually into the proletariat, partly because their diminutive capital does not suffice for the scale on which Modern Industry is carried on, and is swamped in the competition with the large capitalists, partly because their specialized skill is rendered worthless by new méthods of produ¢tion. Thus the proléariat is recruited from all classes of the population.

The proléariat goes through various stages of development. With its birth begins its struggle with the bourgeoisie. At first the contest is carried on by individual laborers, then by the workpeople of a fa¢tory, then by the operatives of one trade, in one locality, against the individual bourgeois who dire¢tly exploits them. They dire¢t their attacks not against the bourgeois conditions of produ¢tion, but against the instruments of produ¢tion themselves; they destroy imported wares that compete with their labor, they smash to pieces machinery, they set fa¢tories ablaze, they seek to restore by force the vanished status of the workman of the Middle Ages.

At this stage the laborers still form an incoherent mass scattered over the whole country, and broken up by their mutual competition. If anywhere they unite to form more compa¢t bodies, this is not yet the consequence of their own a¢tive union, but of the union of the bourgeoisie, which class, in order to attain its own political ends, is compelled to set the whole proletariat in motion, and is moreover yet, for a time, able to do so. At this stage, therefore, the proletarians do not fight their enemies, but the enemies of their enemies, the remnants of absolute monarchy, the landowners, the non-industrial bourgeois, the petty bourgeoisie. Thus the whole historical movement is concentrated in the hands of the bourgeoisie; every victory so obtained is a victory for the bourgeoisie.

But with the development of industry the proletariat not only increases in number, it becomes concentrated in greater masses, its strength grows, and it feels that strength more. The various interests and conditions of life within the ranks of the proletariat are more and more equalized, in proportion as machinery obliterates all distinctions of labor, and nearly everywhere reduces wages to the same low level. The growing competition among the bourgeois, and the resulting commercial crises, make the wages of the workers ever more fluctuating. The unceasing improvement of machinery, ever more rapidly developing, makes their livelihood more and more precarious; the collisions between individual workmen and individual bourgeois take more and more the character of collisions between two classes. Thereupon the workers begin to form combinations (Trades' Unions) against the bourgeois; they club together in order to keep up the rate of wages; they found permanent associations in order to make provision beforehand for these occasional revolts. Here and there the contest breaks out into riots.

Now and then the workers are victorious, but only for a time. The real fruit of their battles lies, not in the immediate result, but in the ever expanding union of the workers. This union is helped on by the improved means of communication that are created by modern industry, and that place the workers of different localities in contact with one another. It was just this contact that was needed to centralize the numerous local struggles, all of the same character, into one national struggle between classes. But every class struggle is a political struggle. And that union, to attain which the burghers of the Middle Ages, with their miserable highways, required centuries, the modern proletarians, thanks to railways, achieve in a few years.

This organization of the proletarians into a class, and consequently into a political party, is continually being upset again by the competition between the workers themselves. But it ever rises up again, stronger, firmer, mightier. It compels legislative recognition of particular interests of the workers by taking advantage of the divisions among the bourgeoisie itself. Thus the ten-hour bill in England was carried.

Altogether collisions between the classes of the old society further, in many ways, the course of development of the proletariat. The bourgeoisie finds itself involved in a constant battle. At first with the aristocracy; later on with those portions of the bourgeoisie itself, whose interests have become antagonistic to the progress of industry; at all times, with the bourgeoisie of foreign countries. In all these battles it sees itself compelled to appeal to the proletariat, to ask for its help, and thus to drag it into the political arena. The bourgeoisie itself, therefore, supplies the proletariat with its own elements of political and general education, in other words, it furnishes the proletariat with weapons for fighting the bourgeoisie.

Further, as we have already seen, entire sections of the ruling classes are, by the advance of industry, precipitated into the proletariat, or are at least threatened in their conditions of existence. These also supply the proletariat with fresh elements of enlightenment and progress.

Finally, in times when the class-struggle nears the decisive hour, the process of dissolution going on within the ruling class, in fact, within the whole range of old society, assumes such a violent, glaring character, that a small section of the ruling class cuts itself adrift, and joins the revolutionary class, the class that holds the future in its hands. Just as, therefore, at an earlier period, a section of the nobility went over to the bourgeoisie, so now a portion of the bourgeoisie goes over to the proletariat, and in particular, a portion of the bourgeois ideologists, who have raised themselves to the level of comprehending theoretically the historical movements as a whole.

Of all the classes that stand face to face with the bourgeoisie today, the proletariat alone is a really revolutionary class. The other classes decay and finally disappear in the face of modern industry; the proletariat is its special and essential product.

The lower middle-class, the small manufacturer, the shopkeeper, the artisan, the peasant, all these fight against the bourgeoisie, to save from extinction their existence as fractions of the middle class. They are, therefore, not revolutionary, but conservative. Nay more, they are reactionary, for they try to roll back the wheel of history. If by chance they are revolutionary, they are so, only in view of their impending transfer into the proletariat, they thus defend not their present, but their future interests, they desert their own standpoint to place themselves at that of the proletariat.

The «dangerous class», the social scum, that passively rotting mass thrown off by the lowest layers of old society, may, here and there, be swept into the movement by a proletarian revolution; its conditions of life, however, prepare it far more for the part of a bribed tool of reactionary intrigue.

In the conditions of the proletariat, those of old society at large are already virtually swamped. The proletarian is without property; his relation to his wife and children has no longer anything in common with the bourgeois family relations; modern industrial labor, modern subjection to capital, the same in England as in France, in America as in Germany, has stripped him of every trace of national character. Law, morality, religion, are to him so many bourgeois prejudices, behind which lurk in ambush just as many bourgeois interests. All the preceding classes that got the upper hand sought to fortify their already acquired status by subjecting society at large to their conditions of appropriation. The proletarians cannot become masters of the productive forces of society, except by abolishing their own previous mode of appropriation, and thereby also every other previous mode of appropriation. They have nothing of their own to secure and to fortify; their mission is to destroy all previous securities for, and insurances of, individual property.

All previous historical movements were movements of minorities, or in the interest of minorities. The proletarian movement is the self-concious, independent movement of the immense majority, in the interest of the immense majority. The proletariat, the lowest stratum of our present society, cannot stir, cannot raise itself up, without the whole superincumbent strata of official society being sprung into the air.

Though not in substance, yet in form, the struggle of the proletariat with the bourgeoisie is at first a national struggle. The proletariat of each country must first of all settle matters with its bourgeoisie.

In depicting the most general phases of the development of the proletariat, we traced the more or less veiled civil war, raging within existing society, up to the point where that war breaks out into open revolution, and where the violent overthrow of the bourgeoisie, lays the foundation for the sway of the proletariat.

Hitherto, every form of society has been based, as we have already seen, on the antagonism of oppressing and oppressed classes. But in order to oppress a class, certain conditions must be assured to it under which it can, at least, continue its slavish existence. The serf, in the period of serfdom, raised himself to membership in the commune, just as the petty bourgeois, under the yoke of feudal absolutism, managed to develop into a bourgeois. The modern laborer, on the contrary, instead of rising with the progress of industry, sinks deeper and deeper below the conditions of existence of his own class. He becomes a pauper, and pauperism develops more rapidly than population and wealth. And here it becomes evident that the bourgeoisie is unfit any longer to be the ruling class in society, and to impose its conditions of existence upon society, as an overriding law. It is unfit to rule, because it is incompetent to assure an existence to its slave within his slavery, because it cannot help letting him sink into such a state that it has to feed him. Society can no longer live under this bourgeoisie, in other words, its existence is no longer compatible with society. The essential condition for the existence, and for the sway of the bourgeois class, is the formation and augmentation of capital; the condition for capital is wage-labor. Wage-labor rests exclusively on competition between the laborers. The advance of industry, whose involuntary promoter is the bourgeoisie, replaces the isolation of the laborers, due to competition, by their involuntary combination, due to association. The development of Modern Industry therefore cuts from under its feet the very foundation on which the bourgeoisie produces and appropriates products. What the bourgeoisie therefore produces, above all, are its own grave-diggers. Its fall and the victory of the proletariat are equally inevitable.

* * *

II PROLETARIANS AND COMMUNISTS

In what relation do the Communists stand to the proletarians as a whole?

The Communists do not form a separate party opposed to other working-class parties.

They have no interests separate and apart from those of the proletariat as a whole.

They do not set up any sectarian principles of their own, by which to shape and mould the proletarian movement.

The Communists are distinguished from the other working-class parties by this only: 1. In the national struggles of the proletarians of the different countries they point out and bring to the front the common interests of the entire proletariat independently of all nationality. 2. In the various stages of development which the struggle of the working class against the bourgeoisie has to pass through, they always and everywhere represent the interests of the movement as a whole.

The Communists, therefore, are on the one hand practically the most advanced and resolute section of the working-class parties of every country, that section which pushes forward all others; on the other hand, theoretically, they have over the great mass of the proletariat the advantage of clearly understanding the line of march, the conditions, and the ultimate general results of the proletarian movement.

The immediate aim of the Communists is the same as that of all the other proletarian parties; formation of the proletariat into a class, overthrow of the bourgeois supremacy, conquest of political power by the proletariat.

The theoretical conclusions of the Communists are in no way based on ideas or principles that have been invented, or discovered, by this or that would-be universal reformer.

They merely express, in general terms, actual relations springing from an existing class struggle, from an historical movement going on under our very eyes. The abolition of existing property relations is not at all a distinctive feature of Communism.

All property relations in the past have continually been subject to historical change consequent upon the change in historical conditions.

The French Revolution, for example, abolished feudal property in favor of bourgeois property.

The distinguishing feature of Communism is not

the abolition of property generally, but the abolition of bourgeois property. But modern bourgeois private property is the final and most complete expression of the system of producing and appropriating products, that is based on class antagonism, on the exploitation of the many by the few.

In this sense, the theory of the Communists may be summed up in the single sentence: Abolition of private property.

We Communists have been reproached with the desire of abolishing the right of personally acquiring property as the fruit of a man's own labor, which property is alleged to be the groundwork of all personal freedom, activity, and independence.

Hard-won, self-acquired, self-earned property! Do you mean the property of the petty artisan and of the small peasant, a form of property that preceded the bourgeois form? There is no need to abolish that; the development of industry has to a great extent already destroyed it, and is still destroying it, daily.

Or do you mean modern bourgeois private property?

But does wage-labor create any property for the laborer? Not a bit. It creates capital, i. e., that kind of property which exploits wage-labor, and which cannot increase except upon condition of getting a new supply of wage-labor for fresh exploitation. Property, in its present form, is based on the antagonism of capital and wage-labor. Let us examine both sides of this antagonism.

To be a capitalist is to have not only a purely personal but a social status in production. Capital is a collective product, and only by the united action of many members, nay, in the last resort, only by the united action of all members of society, can it be set in motion.

Capital is therefore not a personal, it is a social power.

When, therefore, capital is converted into common property, into the property of all members of society, personal property is not thereby transformed into social property. It is only the social character of the property that has changed. It loses its class character. Let us now take wage-labor.

The average price of wage-labor is the minimum wage, i. e., that quantum of the means of subsistence which is absolutely requisite to keep the laborer in bare existence as a laborer. What, therefore, the wage-laborer appropriates by means of his labor, merely suffices to prolong and reproduce a bare existence. We by no means intend to abolish this personal appropriation of the products of labor, an appropriation that is made for the maintenance and reproduction of human life, and that leaves no surplus wherewith to command the labor of others. All that we want to do away with is the miserable character of this appropriation, under which the laborer lives merely to increase capital, and is allowed to live only in so far as the interest of the ruling class requires it.

In bourgeois society, living labor is but a means to increase accumulated labor. In Communist society, accumulated labor is but a means to widen, to enrich, to promote the existence of the laborer.

In bourgeois society, therefore, the past dominates the present; in Communist society, the present dominates the past. In bourgeois society capital is independent and has individuality, while the living person is dependent and has no individuality.

And the abolition of this state of things is called by the bourgeois, abolition of individuality and freedom! And rightly so. The abolition of bourgeois individuality, bourgeois independence, and bourgeois freedom is undoubtedly aimed at.

29

By freedom is meant, under the present bourgeois conditions of production, free trade, free selling and buying.

But if selling and buying disappears, free selling and buying disappears also. This talk about free selling and buying, and all the other «brave words» of our bourgeoisie about freedom in general, have a meaning, if any, only in contrast with restricted selling and buying, with the fettered traders of the Middle Ages, but have no meaning when opposed to the Communist abolition of buying and selling, of the bourgeois conditions of production, and of the bourgeoisie itself.

You are horrified at our intending to do away with private property. But in your existing society, private property is already done away with for nine-tenths of the population; its existence for the few is solely due to its non-existence in the hands of those nine-tenths. You reproach us, therefore, with intending to do away with a form of property, the necessary condition for whose existence is the non-existence of any property for the immense majority of society. In a word, you reproach us with intending to do away with your property. Precisely so; that is just what we intend.

From the moment when labor can no longer be converted into capital, money, or rent, into a social power capable of being monopolized, i.e., from the moment when individual property can no longer be transformed into bourgeois property, into capital, from that moment, you say, individuality vanishes. You must, therefore, confess that by «individual» you mean no other person than the bourgeois, than the middle-class owner of property. This person must, indeed, be swept out of the way, and made impossible.

Communism deprives no man of the power to appropriate the products of society; all that it does is to deprive him of the power to subjugate the labor of others by means of such appropriation.

It has been objected, that upon the abolition of private property all work will cease, and universal laziness will overtake us.

According to this, bourgeois society ought long ago to have gone to the dogs through sheer idleness; for those of its members who work, acquire nothing, and those who acquire anything, do not work. The whole of this objection is but another expression of the tautology: there can no longer be any wage-labor when there is no longer any capital.

All objections urged against the Communistic mode of producing and appropriating material products, have, in the same way, been urged against the Communistic modes of producing and appropriating intellectual products. Just as, to the bourgeois, the disappearance of class property is the disappearance of production itself, so the disappearance of class culture is to him identical with the disappearance of all culture.

That culture, the loss of which he laments, is, for the enormous majority, a mere training to act as a machine.

But don't wrangle with us so long as you apply, to our intended abolition of bourgeois property, the standard of your bourgeois notions of freedom, culture, law, etc. Your very ideas are but the outgrowth of the conditions of your bourgeois production and bourgeois property, just as your jurisprudence is but the will of your class made into a law for all, a will, whose essential character and direction are determined by the economic conditions of existence of your class.

The selfish misconception that induces you to transform into eternal laws of nature and of reason, the social forms springing from your present mode of production and form of property, historical relations that rise and disappear in the progress of production, this misconception you share with every ruling class that has preceded you. What you see clearly in the case of ancient property, what you admit in the case of feudal property, you are of course forbidden to admit in the case of your own bourgeois form of property.

Abolition of the family! Even the most radical flare up at this infamous proposal of the Communists.

On what foundation is the present family, the bourgeois family, based? On capital, on private gain. In its completely developed form this family exists only among the bourgeoisie. But this state of things finds its complement in the practical absence of the family among the proletarians, and in public prostitution.

The bourgeois family will vanish as a matter of course when its complement vanishes, and both will vanish with the vanishing of capital.

Do you charge us with wanting to stop the exploitation of children by their parents? To this crime we plead guilty.

But, you will say, we destroy the most hallowed of relations, when we replace home education by social.

And your education! Is not that also social, and determined by the social conditions under which you educate, by the intervention, direct or indirect, of society by means of schools, etc.? The Communists have not invented the intervention of society in education; they do but seek to alter the character of that intervention, and to rescue education from the influence of the ruling class.

The bourgeois clap-trap about the family and education, about the hallowed co-relation of parent and child, becomes all the more disgusting, the more, by the action of Modern Industry, all family ties among the proletarians are torn asunder, and their children transformed into simple articles of commerce and instruments of labor.

But you Communists would introduce community of women, screams the whole bourgeoisie in chorus. The bourgeois sees in his wife a mere instrument of production. He hears that the instruments of production are to be exploited in common, and, naturally, can come to no other conclusion than that the lot of being common to all will likewise fall to the women.

He has not even a suspicion that the real point aimed at is to do away with the status of women as the mere instruments of production in society. For the rest, nothing is more ridiculous than the virtuous indignation of our bourgeois at the community of women which, they pretend, is to be openly and officially established by the Communists. The Communists have no need to introduce community of women; it has existed almost from time immemorial.

Our bourgeois, not content with having the wives and daughters of their proletarians at their disposal, not to speak of the common prostitutes, take the greatest pleasure in seducing each others' wives.

Bourgeois marriage is in reality a system of wives in common and thus, at the most, what the Communists might possibly be reproached with, is that they desire to introduce, in substitution for a hypocritically concealed, an openly legalized community of women. For the rest, it is self-evident that the abolition of the present system of production must bring with it the abolition of the community of women springing from that system, i. e., of prostitution both public and private.

The Communists are further reproached with desiring to abolish countries and nationalities.

The working men have no country. We cannot take

from them what they have not got. Since the proletariat must first of all acquire political supremacy, must rise to be the leading class of the nation, must constitute itself the nation, it is, so far, itself national, though not in the bourgeois sense of the word.

The national differences and antagonisms between peoples are daily more and more vanishing, owing to the development of the bourgeoisie, to freedom of commerce, to the world-market, to uniformity in the mode of production and in the conditions of life corresponding thereto.

The supremacy of the proletariat will cause them to vanish still faster. United action, of the leading civilized countries at least, is one of the first conditions for the emancipation of the proletariat.

In proportion as the exploitation of one individual by another is put an end to, the exploitation of one nation by another will also be put an end to. In proportion as the antagonism between classes within the nation vanishes, the hostility of one nation to another will come to an end.

The charges against Communism made from a religious, a philosophical, and generally, from an ideological standpoint, are not deserving of serious examination.

Does it require deep intuition to comprehend that man's ideas, views, and conceptions, in one word, man's consciousness, changes with every change in the conditions of his material existence, in his social relations and in his social life?

What else does the history of ideas prove, than that intellectual production changes in character in proportion as material production is changed? The ruling ideas of each age have ever been the ideas of its ruling class.

When people speak of ideas that revolutionize society, they do but express the fact, that within the old society, the elements of a new one have been created, and that the dissolution of the old ideas keeps even pace with the dissolution of the old conditions of existence.

When the ancient world was in its last throes, the ancient religions were overcome by Christianity. When Christian ideas succumbed in the 18th century to rationalist ideas, feudal society fought its death battle with the then revolutionary bourgeoisie. The ideas of religious liberty and freedom of conscience, merely gave expression to the sway of free competition within the domain of knowledge. "Undoubtedly," it will be said, "religious, moral, philosophical and juridical ideas have been modified in the course of historical development. But religion, morality, philosophy, political science, and law, constantly survived this change."

"There are, besides, eternal truths, such as Freedom, Justice, etc., that are common to all states of society. But Communism abolishes eternal truths, it abolishes all religion, and all morality, instead of constituting them on a new basis; it therefore acts in contradiction to all past historical experience."

What does this accusation reduce itself to? The history of all past society has consisted in the development of class antagonisms, antagonisms that assumed different forms at different epochs.

But whatever form they may have taken, one fact is common to all past ages, viz., the exploitation of one part of society by the other. No wonder, then, that the social consciousness of past ages, despite all the multiplicity and variety it displays, moves within certain common forms, or general ideas, which cannot completely vanish except with the total disappearance of class antagonisms.

The Communist revolution is the most radical rupture with traditional property relations; no wonder its development involves the most radical rupture with the traditional ideas of all of the bourgeoisie. But let us have done with the bourgeois objections to Communism.

We have seen above, that the first step in the revolution by the working class, is to raise the proletariat to the position of ruling class, to win the battle of democracy.

The proletariat will use its political supremacy to wrest, by degrees, all capital from the bourgeoisie, to centralize all instruments of production in the hands of the State, i. e., of the proletariat organized as the ruling class, and to increase the total of productive forces as rapidly as possible.

Of course, in the beginning, this cannot be effected except by means of despotic inroads on the rights of property, and on the conditions of bourgeois production; by means of measures, therefore, which appear economically insufficient and untenable, but which, in the course of the movement, outstrip themselves, necessitate further inroads upon the old social order, and are unavoidable as a means of entirely revolutionizing the mode of production.

These measures will of course be different in different countries.

Nevertheless in the most advanced countries the

following will be found pretty generally applicable:

1. Abolition of property in land and application of all rents of land to public purposes.

2. A heavy progressive or graduated income tax.

3. Abolition of all right of inheritance.

4. Confiscation of property of emigrants and rebels.

5. Centralization of credit in the hands of the State, by means of a national bank with State capital and an exclusive monopoly.

6. Centralization of the means of communication and transport in the hands of the State.

7. Extension of factories and instruments of production owned by the State; the bringing into cultivation of waste lands, and the improvement of the soil generally in accordance with a common plan.

8. Equal liability of all to labor. Establishment of industrial armies, especially for agriculture.

9. Combination of agriculture with manufacturing industries; gradual abolition of the distinction between town and country, by a more equable distribution of population over the country.

10. Free education for all children in public schools. Abolition of children's factory labor in its present form. Combination of education with industrial production, etc., etc.

When, in the course of development, class distinctions have disappeared, and all production has been concentrated in the hands of a vast association of the whole nation, the public power will lose its political character. Political power, properly so called, is merely the organized power of one class for oppressing another. If the proletariat during its contest with the bourgeoisie is compelled, by the force of circumstances, to organize itself as a class, if, by means of a revolution, it makes itself the ruling class, and, as such, sweeps away by force the old conditions of production, then it will, along with these conditions, have swept away the conditions for the existence of class antagonisms, and of classes generally, and will thereby have abolished its own supremacy as a class.

In place of the old bourgeois society, with its classes and class antagonisms, we shall have an association, in which the free development of each is the condition for the free development of all.

* ** *

III SOCIALIST AND COMMUNIST LITERATURE

1 Reactionary Socialism

a Feudal Socialism

Owing to their historical position, it became the vocation of the aristocracies of France and England to write pamphlets against modern bourgeois society. In the French revolution of July, 1830, and in the English reform agitation, these aristocracies again succumbed to the hateful upstart. Thenceforth, a serious political contest was altogether out of the question. A literary battle alone remained possible. But even in the domain of literature the old cries of the restoration period had become impossible.

In order to arouse sympathy, the aristocracy were obliged to lose sight, apparently, of their own interests, and to formulate their indictment against the bourgeoisie in the interest of the exploited working class alone. Thus the aristocracy took their revenge by singing lampoons on their new master, and whispering in his ears sinister prophecies of coming catastrophe.

In this way arose feudal socialism; half lamentation,

half lampoon; half echo of the past, half menace of the future; at times, by its bitter, witty, and incisive criticism, striking the bourgeoisie to the very hearts' core, but always ludicrous in its effect, through total incapacity to comprehend the march of modern history.

The aristocracy, in order to rally the people to them, waved the proletarian alms-bag in front for a banner. But the people, so often as it joined them, saw on their hindquarters the old feudal coats of arms, and deserted with loud and irreverent laughter.

One section of the French Legitimists, and "Young England," exhibited this spectacle.

In pointing out that their mode of exploitation was different to that of the bourgeoisie, the feudalists forget that they exploited under circumstances and conditions that were quite different, and that are now antiquated. In showing that, under their rule, the modern proletariat never existed, they forget that the modern bourgeoisie is the necessary off-spring of their own form of society.

For the rest, so little do they conceal the reactionary character of their criticism, that their chief accusation against the bourgeoisie amounts to this, that under the bourgeois regime a class is being developed, which is destined to cut up root and branch the old order of society.

What they upbraid the bourgeoisie with is not so much that it creates a proletariat, as that it creates a revolutionary proletariat.

In political practice, therefore, they join in all coercive measures against the working-class; and in ordinary life, despite their high falutin phrases, they stoop to pick up the golden apples dropped from the tree of industry, and to barter truth, love, and honor for traffic in wool, beetroot-sugar and potato spirit.

As the parson has ever gone hand in hand with the landlord, so has Clerical Socialism gone along with Feudal Socialism.

Nothing is easier than to give Christian asceticism a Socialist tinge. Has not Christianity declaimed against private property, against marriage, against the State? Has it not preached in the place of these charity and poverty, celibacy, and mortification of the flesh, monastic life and Mother Church? Christian Socialism is but the Holy Water with which the priest consecrates the heart-burnings of the aristocrat.

* * *

b Petty Bourgeois Socialism

The feudal aristocracy was not the only class that was ruined by the bourgeoisie, not the only class whose conditions of existence pined and perished in the atmosphere of modern bourgeois society. The medieval burgesses and the small peasant bourgeoisie, were the precursors of the modern bourgeoisie. In those countries which are but little developed, industrially and commercially, these two classes still vegetate side by side with the rising bourgeoisie.

In countries where modern civilization has become fully developed, a new class of petty bourgeois has been formed, fluctuating between proletariat and bourgeoisie, and ever renewing itself as a supplementary part of bourgeois society. The individual members of this class, however, are being constantly hurled down into the proletariat by the action of competition, and, as modern industry develops, they even see the moment approaching when they will completely disappear as an independent section of modern society, to be replaced, in manufactures, agriculture and commerce, by overlookers, bailiffs and shopmen.

In countries like France, where the peasants constitute far more than half of the population, it was natural that writers who sided with the proletariat against the bourgeoisie, should use, in their criticism of the bourgeoisie regime, the standard of the peasant and petty bourgeois, and from the standpoint of these intermediate classes should take up the cudgels for the working-class. Thus arose petty bourgeois Socialism. Sismondi was the head of this school, not only in France, but also in England.

This school of Socialism dissected with great acuteness the contradictions in the conditions of modern production. It laid bare the hypocritical apologies of economists. It proved, incontrovertibly, the disastrous effects of machinery and division of labor; the concentration of capital and land in a few hands; overproduction and crises; it pointed out the inevitable ruin of the petty bourgeois and peasant, the misery of the proletariat, the anarchy in production, the crying inequalities in the distribution of wealth, the industrial war of extermination between nations, the dissolution of old moral bonds, of the old family relations, of the old nationalities.

In its positive aims, however, this form of Socialism aspires either to restoring the old means of production and of exchange, and with them the old property relations, and the old society, or to cramping the modern means of production and of exchange, within the framework of the old property relations that have been, and were bound to be, exploded by those means. In either case, it is both reactionary and Utopian.

Its last words are: corporate guilds for manufacture; patriarchal relations in agriculture.

Ultimately, when stubborn historical facts had dispersed all intoxicating effects of self-deception, this form of Socialism ended in a miserable fit of the blues.

German or «True» Socialism

The Socialist and Communist literature of France, a literature that originated under the pressure of a bourgeoisie in power, and that was the expression of the struggle against this power, was introduced into Germany at a time when the bourgeoisie, in that country, had just begun its contest with feudal absolutism.

German philosophers, would-be philosophers, and beaux esprits, eagerly seized on this literature, only forgetting this, that when these writings emigrated from France into Germany, French social conditions had not emigrated along with them. In contact with German social conditions, this French literature lost all its immediate practical significance, and assumed a purely literary aspect. Thus, to the German philosophers of the eighteenth century, the demands of the first French Revolution were nothing more than the demands of «Practical Reason» in general, and the utterance of the will of the revolutionary French bourgeoisie signified in their eyes the laws of pure Will, of Will as it was bound to be, of true human Will generally.

The work of the German literati consisted solely in bringing the new French ideas into harmony with their ancient philosophical conscience, or rather in annexing the French ideas without deserting their own philosophic point of view.

This annexation took place in the same way in which a foreign language is appropriated, by translation. It is well known how the monks wrote silly lives of Catholic saints over the manuscripts on which the classical works of ancient heathendom had been written. The German literati reversed this process with the profane French literature. They wrote their philosophical nonsense beneath the French original. For instance, beneath the French criticism of the economic functions of money, they wrote, "Alienation of Humanity," and beneath the French criticism of the bourgeois State they wrote, "Dethronement of the Category of the General," and so forth.

The introduction of these philosophical phrases at the back of the French historical criticisms they dubbed "Philosophy of Action," "True Socialism," "German Science of Socialism," "Philosophical Foundation of Socialism," and so on.

The French Socialist and Communist literature was thus completely emasculated. And, since it ceased in the hands of the German to express the struggle of one class with the other, he felt conscious of having overcome "French one-sidedness" and of representing, not true requirements, but the requirements of Truth, not the interests of the proletariat, but the interests of Human Nature, of Man in general, who belongs to no class, has no reality, who exists only in the realm of philosophical phantasy. This German Socialism, which took its schoolboy task so seriously and solemnly, and extolled its poor stock-in-trade in such mountebank fashion, meanwhile gradually lost its pedantic innocence.

The fight of the German, and, especially, of the Prussian bourgeoisie, against feudal aristocracy and absolute monarchy, in other words, the liberal movement, became more earnest.

By this, the long-wished-for opportunity was offered to «True Socialism» of confronting the political movement with the socialist demands of hurling the traditional anathemas against liberalism, against representative government, against bourgeois competition, bourgeois freedom of the press, bourgeois legislation, bourgeois liberty and equality, and of preaching to the masses that they had nothing to gain and everything to lose by this bourgeois movement. German Socialism forgot, in the nick of time, that the French criticism, whose silly echo it was, presupposed the existence of modern bourgeois society, with its corresponding economic conditions of existence, and the political constitution adapted thereto, the very things whose attainment was the object of the pending struggle in Germany.

To the absolute governments, with their following of parsons, professors, country squires and officials, it served as more than a welcome scarecrow against the threatening bourgeoisie.

It was a sweet finish after the bitter pills of floggings and bullets, with which these same governments, just at that time, dosed the German working-class risings.

While this True Socialism thus served the governments as a weapon for fighting the German bourgeoisie, it at the same time directly represented a reactionary interest, the interest of the German Philistines. In Germany the petty bourgeois class, a relic of the sixteenth century, and since then constantly cropping up again under various forms, is the real social basis of the existing state of things.

To preserve this class is to preserve the existing state of things in Germany. The industrial and political supremacy of the bourgeoisie threatens it with certain destruction; on the one hand from the concentration of capital; on the other from the rise of a revolutionary proletariat. True Socialism appeared to kill these two birds with one stone. It spread like an epidemic.

The robe of speculative cobwebs, embroidered with flowers of rhetoric, steeped in the dew of sickly sentiment, this transcendental robe in which the German Socialists wrapped their sorry eternal truths, all skin and bone, served wonderfully to increase the sale of their goods amongst such a public.

And on its part, German Socialism recognized more and more its own calling as the bombastic representative of the petty bourgeois Philistine.

It proclaimed the German nation to be the model

nation, and the German petty Philistine to be the typical man. To every villainous meanness of this model man it gave a hidden, higher, socialistic interprétation, the exact contrary of its true character. It went to the extreme length of directly opposing the «brutally destructive» tendency of Communism, and of proclaiming its supreme and impartial contempt of all class struggles. With very few exceptions, all the so-called Socialist and Communist publications that now (1847) circulate in Germany belong to the domain of this foul and enervating literature.

2 Conservative or Bourgeois Socialism

A part of the bourgeoisie is desirous of redressing social grievances in order to secure the continued existence of bourgeois society.

To this section belong economists, philanthropists, humanitarians, improvers of the condition of the work class, organizers of charity, members of societies for the prevention of cruelty to animals, temperance fanatics, hole and corner reformers of every imaginable kind. This form of Socialism has, moreover, been worked out into complete systems.

We may cite Proudhon's «Philosophie de la Misere» as an example of this form.

The socialistic bourgeois want all the advantages of modern social conditions without the struggles and dangers necessarily resulting therefrom. They desire the existing state of society minus its revolutionary and disintegrating elements. They wish for a bourgeoisie without a proletariat. The bourgeoisie naturally conceives the world in which it is supreme to be the best; and bourgeois Socialism develops this comfortable conception into various more or less complete systems. In requiring the proletariat to carry out such a system, and thereby to march straightway into the social New Jerusalem, it but requires in reality, that the proletariat should remain within the bounds of existing society, but should cast away all its hateful ideas about the bourgeoisie. A second and more practical, but less systematic, form of this Socialism sought to depreciate every revolutionary movement in the eyes of the working class, by showing that no mere political reform, but only a change in the material conditions of existence, in economical relations, could be of any advantage to them. By changes in the material conditions of existence, this form of Socialism, however, by no means understands abolition of the bourgeois relations of production, an abolition that can be effected only by a revolution, but administrative reforms, based on the continued existence of these relations; reforms, therefore, that in no respect affect the relations between capital and labor, but, at the best, lessen the cost and simplify the administrative work of bourgeois government.

Bourgeois Socialism attains adequate expression, when, and only when, it becomes a mere figure of speech.

Free trade: for the benefit of the working class. Protective duties: for the benefit of the working class. Prison Reform: for the benefit of the working class. These are the last words and the only seriously meant words of bourgeois Socialism.

It is summed up in the phrase: the bourgeois are bourgeois for the benefit of the working class.

3 Critical-Utopian Socialism and Communism

We do not here refer to that literature which in every great modern revolution has always given voice to the demands of the proletariat, such as the writings of Babeuf and others.

The first direct attempts of the proletariat to attain its own ends were made in times of universal excitement when feudal society was being overthrown. These attempts necessarily failed, owing to the then undeveloped state of the proletariat, as well as to the absence of the economic conditions for its emancipation, conditions that had yet to be produced, and could be produced by the impending bourgeois epoch alone. The revolutionary literature that accompanied these first movements of the proletariat had necessarily a reactionary character. It inculcated universal asceticism and social leveling in its crudest form.

The Socialist and Communist systems properly so-called, those of St. Simon, Fourier, Owen, and others, spring to existence in the early undeveloped period, described above, of the struggle between proletariat and bourgeoisie (see I Bourgeoisie and Proletariat). The founders of these systems see, indeed, the class antagonisms, as well as the action of the decomposing elements in the prevailing form of society. But the proletariat, as yet in its infancy, offers to them the spectacle of a class without any historical initiative or any independent political movement. Since the development of class antagonism keeps even pace with the development of industry, the economic situation, as they find it, does not as yet offer to them the material conditions for the emancipation of the proletariat. They therefore search after a new social science, after new social laws, that are to create these conditions.

Historical action is to yield to their personal inventive action; historically created conditions of emancipation to fantastic ones; and the gradual, spontaneous class organization of the proletariat to an organization of society specially contrived by these inventors. Future history resolves itself, in their eyes, into the propaganda and the practical carrying out of their social plans.

In the formation of their plans they are concious of caring chiefly for the interests of the working class, as being the most suffering class. Only from the point of view of being the most suffering class does the proletariat exist for them.

The undeveloped state of the class struggle, as well as their own surroundings, cause Socialists of this kind to consider themselves far superior to all class antagonisms. They want to improve the condition of every member of society, even that of the most favored. Hence, they habitually appeal to society at large, without distinction of class; nay, by preference, to the ruling class. For how can people, when once they understand their system, fail to see in it the best possible plan of the best state of society?

Hence, they reject all political and especially all revolutionary action; they wish to attain their ends by peaceful means, and endeavor by small experiments, necessarily doomed to failure, and by the force of example to pave their way for the new social Gospel. Such fantastic pictures of future society, painted at a time when the proletariat is still in a very undeveloped state and has but a fantastic conception of its own position, correspond with the first instinctive yearnings of that class for a general reconstruction of society.

But these Socialist and Communist publications contain also a critical element. They attack every principle of existing society. Hence they are full of the most valuable materials for the enlightenment of the working class. The practical measures proposed in them, such as the abolition of the distinction between town and country, of the family, of the carrying on of industries for the account of private individuals, and of the wage system, the proclamation of social harmony, the conversion of the functions of the State into a mere superintendence of production, all these proposals point solely to the disappearance of class antagonisms which were, at that time, only just cropping up, and which, in these publications, are recognized under their earliest, indistinct and undefined forms only. These proposals therefore are of a purely Utopian character.

The significance of Critical-Utopian Socialism and Communism bears an inverse relation to historical development. In proportion as the modern class struggle develops and takes definite shape, this fantastic standing apart from the contest, these fantastic attacks on it lose all practical value and all theoretical justification. Therefore, although the originators of these systems were, in many respects, revolutionary, their disciples have, in every case, formed mere reactionary sects. They hold fast by the original views of their masters, in opposition to the progressive historical development of the proletariat. They endeavor, therefore, and that consistently, to deaden the class struggle and to reconcile the class antagonisms. They still dream of experimental realization of their social Utopias, of founding isolated «phalansteres», of establishing «Home Colonies», of setting up a «Little Icaria», duodecimo editions of the New Jerusalem, and to realize all these castles in the air, they are compelled to appeal to the feelings and purses of the bourgeois. By degrees they sink into the category of the reactionary conservative

Socialists depicted above, differing from these only by more systematic pedantry, and by their fanatical and superstitious belief in the miraculous effects of their social science.

They, therefore, violently oppose all political action on the part of the working class; such action, according to them, can only result from blind unbelief in the new Gospel.

The Owenites in England, and the Fourierists in France, respectively, oppose the Chartists and the «Reformistes».

* * *

I V POSITION OF THE COMMUNISTS IN RELATION TO THE VARIOUS EXISTING OPPOSITION PARTIES

Section II has made clear the relations of the Communists to existing working-class parties, such as the Chartists in England and the Agrarian Reformers in America.

The Communists are constantly fighting for the attainment of the immediate aims for the enforcement of the interests of the working class; but in the movement of the present, they also represent and take care of the future of that movement. In France the Communists ally themselves with the Social-Democrats against the conservative and radical bourgeoisie, reserving, however, the right to take up a critical position in regard to phrases and illusions traditionally handed down from the great Revolution.

In Switzerland they support the Radicals without losing sight of the fact that this party consists of antagonistic elements, partly of Democratic Socialists, in the French sense, partly of radical bourgeois.

In Poland they support the party that insists on an agrarian revolution, as the prime condition for national emancipation, that party which fomented the insurrection at Cracow in 1846.

In Germany they fight with the bourgeoisie whenever it acts in a revolutionary way, against the absolute monarchy, the feudal squirearchy, and the petty bourgeoisie.

But they never cease, for a single instant, to instill into the working class the clearest possible recognition of the hostile antagonism between bourgeoisie and proletariat, in order that the German workers may straightway use, as so many weapons against the bourgeoisie, the social and political conditions that the bourgeoisie must necessarily introduce along with its supremacy, and in order that, after the fall of the reactionary classes in Germany, the fight against the bourgeoisie itself may immediately begin.

The Communists turn their attention chiefly to Germany, because that country is on the eve of a bourgeois revolution that is bound to be carried out under more advanced conditions of European civilization and with a more developed proletariat than existed in England in the seventeenth, and in France in the eighteenth century, and because the bourgeois revolution in Germany will be but the prelude to an immediately following proletarian revolution. In short, the Communists everywhere support every revolutionary movement against the existing social and political order of things.

In all these movements they bring to the front, as the leading question in each, the property question, no matter what its degree of development at that time.

Finally, they labor everywhere for the union and agreement of the democratic parties of all countries. The Communists disdain to conceal their views and aims. They openly declare that their ends can be attained only by the forcible overthrow of all existing social conditions. Let the ruling classes tremble at a Communistic revolution. The proletarians have nothing to lose but their chains. They have a world to win.

Working men of all countries, unite!

* * *

PRINCIPLES
OF
COMMUNISM

Friedrich Engels

PRINCIPLES OF COMMUNISM

QUESTION 1.　WHAT IS COMMUNISM?

ANSWER. Communism is the doctrine of the conditions of the liberation of the proletariat.

QUESTION 2.　WHAT IS THE PROLETARIAT?

ANSWER. The proletariat is that class in society which lives entirely from the sale of its labor and does not draw profit from any kind of capital; whose weal and woe, whose life and death, whose whole existence depends on the demand for labor, hence on the changing state of business, on the vagaries of unbridled competition. The proletariat, or the class of proletarians, is, in a word, the working class of the nineteenth century.

QUESTION 3.　PROLETARIANS, THEN, HAVE NOT
ALWAYS EXISTED?

ANSWER. No. There have always been poor and working classes; and the working classes have mostly been poor. But there have not always been workers and poor people living under conditions as they are today; in other words, there have not always been proletarians, any more than there has always been free unbridled competition.

ANSWER. The proletariat originated in the industrial revolution which took place in England in the last half of the last [eighteenth] century, and which has since then been repeated in all the civilized countries of the world. This industrial revolution was precipitated by the discovery of the steam engine, various spinning machines, the mechanical loom, and a whole series of other mechanical devices. These machines, which were very expensive and hence could be bought only by big capitalists, altered the whole mode of production and displaced the former workers, because the machines turned out cheaper and better commodities than the workers could produce with their inefficient spinning wheels and handlooms. The machines delivered industry wholly into the hands of the big capitalists and rendered entirely worthless the meager property of the workers (tools, looms, etc.). The result was that the capitalists soon had everything in their hands and nothing remained to the workers. This marked the introduction of the factory system into the textile industry.

Once the impulse to the introduction of machinery and the factory system had been given, this system spread quickly to all other branches of industry, especially cloth- and book-printing, pottery, and the metal industries. Labor was more and more divided among the individual workers so that the worker who previously had done a complete piece of work now did only part of that piece. This division of labor made it possible to produce things faster and cheaper. It reduced the activity of the individual worker to simple, endlessly repeated mechanical motions which could be performed not only as well but much better by a machine. In this way, all these industries fell, one after another, under the dominance of steam, machinery, and the factory system, just as spinning and weaving had already done. But at the same time they also fell into the hands of big capitalists, and their workers were deprived of whatever independence remained to them. Gradually, not only genuine manufacture but also handicrafts came within the province of the factory system as big capitalists increasingly displaced the small master craftsmen by setting up huge workshops which saved many expenses and permitted an elaborate division of labor.

This is how it has come about that in civilized countries at the present time nearly all kinds of labor are performed in factories, and in nearly all branches of work handicrafts and manufacture have been superseded. This process has to an ever greater degree ruined the old middle class, especially the small handicraftsmen; it has entirely transformed the condition of the workers; and two new classes have been created which are gradually swallowing up all the others. These are:

(1) The class of big capitalists, who in all civilized countries are already in almost exclusive possession of all the means of subsistence and of the instruments (machines, factories) and the materials necessary for the production of the means of subsistence. This is the bourgeois class, or the bourgeoisie.

(2) The class of the wholly propertyless, who are obliged to sell their labor to the bourgeoisie in order to get in exchange the means of subsistence necessary for their support. This is called the class of proletarians, or the proletariat.

QUESTION 5. UNDER WHAT CONDITIONS DOES THIS
SALE OF THE LABOR OF THE PROLETARIANS
TO THE BOURGEOISIE TAKE PLACE?

ANSWER. Labor is a commodity like any other and its price is therefore determined by exactly the same laws that apply to other commodities. In a regime of big industry or of free competition—as we shall see, the two come to the same thing—the price of a commodity is on the average always equal to its costs of production. Hence the price of labor is also equal to the costs of production of labor. But the costs of production of labor consist of precisely the quantity of means of subsistence necessary to enable the worker to continue working and to prevent the working class from dying out. The worker will therefore get no more for his labor than is necessary for this purpose; the price of labor or the wage will, in other words, be the lowest, the minimum, required for the maintenance of life. However, since business is sometimes better and sometimes worse, it follows that the worker sometimes gets more and sometimes less, just as the industrialist sometimes gets more and sometimes less for his commodities. But again, just as the industrialist, on the average of good times and bad, gets no more and no less for his commodities than what they cost, similarly on the average the worker gets no more and no less than this minimum. This economic law of wages operates the more strictly the greater the degree to which big industry has taken possession of all branches of production.

QUESTION 6. WHAT WORKING CLASSES WERE THERE
BEFORE THE INDUSTRIAL REVOLUTION?

ANSWER. The working classes have always, according to the different stages of development of society, lived in different circumstances and had different relations to the owning and ruling classes. In antiquity, the workers were the *slaves* of the owners, just as they still are in many backward countries and even in the southern part of the United States. In the Middle Ages, they were the *serfs* of the landowning nobility, as they still are in Hungary, Poland, and Russia. In the Middle Ages, and indeed right up to the industrial revolution, there were also journeymen in the cities who worked in the service of petty bourgeois masters. Gradually, as manufacture developed, these journeymen became manufacturing workers who were even then employed by larger capitalists.

QUESTION 7. In what way do proletarians differ from slaves?

ANSWER. The slave is sold once and for all; the proletarian must sell himself daily and hourly. The individual slave, property of one master, is assured an existence, however miserable it may be, because of the master's interest. The individual proletarian, property as it were of the entire bourgeois class which buys his labor only when someone has need of it, has no secure existence. This existence is assured only to the *class* as a whole. The slave is outside competition; the proletarian is in it and experiences all its vagaries. The slave counts as a thing, not as a member of civil society; the proletarian is recognized as a person, as a member of civil society. Thus the slave can have a better existence than the proletarian, while the proletarian belongs to a higher stage of social development and himself stands on a higher social level than the slave. The slave frees himself when, of all the relations of private property, he abolishes only the relation of slavery and thereby becomes a proletarian; the proletarian can free himself only by abolishing private property in general.

QUESTION 8. In what way do proletarians differ from serfs?

ANSWER. The serf possesses and uses an instrument of production, a piece of land, in exchange for which he gives up a part of his product or part of the services of his labor. The proletarian works with the instruments of production of another, for the account of this other, in exchange for a part of the product. The serf gives up, the proletarian receives. The serf has an assured existence, the proletarian has not. The serf is outside competition, the proletarian is in it. The serf liberates himself in one of three ways: either he runs away to the city and there becomes a handicraftsman; or, instead of products and services, he gives money to his lord and thereby becomes a free tenant; or he overthrows his feudal lord and himself becomes a property owner. In short, by one route or another he gets into the owning class and enters into competition. The proletarian liberates himself by abolishing competition, private property, and all class differences.

QUESTION 9.   IN WHAT WAY DO PROLETARIANS DIFFER
FROM HANDICRAFTSMEN?

QUESTION 10.   IN WHAT WAY DO PROLETARIANS DIFFER
FROM MANUFACTURING WORKERS?

ANSWER. The manufacturing worker of the sixteenth to the eighteenth centuries still had, with but few exceptions, an instrument of production in his own possession—his loom, the family spinning wheel, a little plot of land which he cultivated in his spare time. The proletarian has none of these things. The manufacturing worker almost always lives in the countryside and in a more or less patriarchal relation to his landlord or employer; the proletarian lives for the most part in the city and his relation to his employer is purely a cash relation. The manufacturing worker is torn out of his patriarchal relation by big industry, loses whatever property he still has, and in this way becomes a proletarian.

QUESTION 11.   WHAT WERE THE IMMEDIATE
CONSEQUENCES OF THE INDUSTRIAL
REVOLUTION AND OF THE DIVISION
OF SOCIETY INTO BOURGEOISIE
AND PROLETARIAT?

ANSWER. *First*, the lower and lower prices of industrial products brought about by machine labor totally destroyed in all countries of the world the old system of manufacture or industry based upon hand labor. In this way, all semi-barbarian countries, which had hitherto been more or less strangers to historical development and whose industry had been based on manufacture, were violently forced out of their isolation. They bought the cheaper commodities of the English and allowed their own manufacturing workers to be ruined. Countries which had known no progress for thousands of years, for example India, were thoroughly revolutionized, and even China is now on the way to a revolution. We have come to the point where a new machine invented in England deprives millions of Chinese workers of their livelihood within a year's time. In this way big industry has brought all the people of the earth into contact with each other, has merged all local markets into one world market, has spread civilization and progress everywhere and has thus ensured that whatever happens in the civilized countries will have repercussions in all other countries. It follows that if the workers in England or France now liberate themselves, this must set off revolutions in all other countries—revolutions which sooner or later must accomplish the liberation of their respective working classes.

Second, wherever big industries displaced manufacture, the bourgeoisie developed in wealth and power to the utmost and made itself the first class of the country. The result was that wherever this happened the bourgeoisie took political power into its own hands and displaced the hitherto ruling classes, the aristocracy, the guildmasters, and their representative, the absolute monarchy. The bourgeoisie annihilated the power of the aristocracy, the nobility, by abolishing the entailment of estates, in other words by making landed property subject to purchase and sale, and by doing away with the special privileges of the nobility. It destroyed the power of the guildmasters by abolishing guilds and handicraft privileges. In their place, it put competition, that is, a state of society in which everyone has the right to enter into any branch of industry, the only obstacle being a lack of the necessary capital. The introduction of free competition is thus a public declaration that from now on the members of society are unequal only to the extent that their capitals are unequal, that capital is the decisive power, and that therefore the capitalists, the bourgeoisie, have become the first class in society.

Free competition is necessary for the establishment of big industry, because it is the only condition of society in which big industry can make its way. Having destroyed the social power of the nobility and the guildmasters, the bourgeoisie also destroyed their political power. Having raised itself to the actual position of first class in society, it proclaims itself to be also the dominant political class. This it does through the introduction of the representative system which rests on bourgeois equality before the law and the recognition of free competition, and in European countries takes the form of constitutional monarchy. In these constitutional monarchies, only those who possess a certain capital are voters, that is to say, only members of the bourgeoisie. These bourgeois voters choose the deputies, and these bourgeois deputies, by using their right to refuse to vote taxes, choose a bourgeois government.

Third, everywhere the proletariat develops in step with the bourgeoisie. In proportion as the bourgeoisie grows in wealth the proletariat grows in numbers. For, since proletarians can be employed only by capital, and since capital expands only through employing labor, it follows that the growth of the proletariat proceeds at precisely the same pace as the growth of capital. Simultaneously, this process draws members of the bourgeoisie and proletarians together into the great cities where industry can be carried on most profitably, and by thus throwing great masses in one spot it gives to the proletarians a consciousness of their own strength. Moreover, the further this process advances, the more new labor-saving machines are invented, the greater is the pressure exercised by big industry on wages, which, as we have seen, sink to their minimum and therewith render the condition of the proletariat increasingly unbearable. The growing dissatisfaction of the proletariat thus joins with its rising power to prepare a proletarian social revolution.

QUESTION 12. WHAT WERE THE FURTHER CONSEQUENCES OF THE INDUSTRIAL REVOLUTION?

ANSWER. Big industry created in the steam engine and other machines the means of endlessly expanding industrial production, speeding it up, and cutting its costs. With production thus facilitated, the free competition which is necessarily bound up with big industry assumed the most extreme forms; a multitude of capitalists invaded industry, and in a short while more was produced than was needed. As a consequence, finished commodities could not be sold, and a so-called commercial crisis broke out. Factories had to be closed, their owners went bankrupt, and the workers were without bread. Deepest misery reigned everywhere. After a time, the superfluous products were sold, the factories began to operate again, wages rose, and gradually business got better than ever. But it was not long before too many commodities were again produced and a new crisis broke out, only to follow the same course as its predecessor. Ever since the beginning of this [nineteenth] century, the condition of industry has constantly fluctuated between periods of prosperity and periods of crisis; nearly every five to seven years a fresh crisis has intervened, always with the greatest hardship for workers, and always accompanied by general revolutionary stirrings and the direst peril to the whole existing order of things.

QUESTION 13. WHAT FOLLOWS FROM THESE PERIODIC COMMERCIAL CRISES?

ANSWER. *First:* That though big industry in its earliest stage created free competition, it has now outgrown free competition; that for big industry competition and generally the individualistic organization of production have become a fetter which it must and will shatter; that so long as big industry remains on its present footing it can be maintained only at the cost of general chaos every seven years, each time threatening the whole of civilization and not only plunging the proletarians into misery but also ruining large sections of the bourgeoisie; hence either that big industry must itself be given up, which is an absolute impossibility, or that it makes unavoidably necessary an entirely new organization of society in which production is no longer directed by mutually competing individual industrialists but rather by the whole society operating according to a definite plan and taking account of the needs of all.

Second: That big industry and the limitless expansion of production which it makes possible bring within the range of feasibility a social order in which so much is produced that every member of society will be in a position to exercise and develop all his powers and faculties in complete freedom. It thus appears that the very qualities of big industry which in our present-day society produce misery and crises are those which in a different form of society will abolish this misery and these catastrophic depressions. We see with the greatest clarity:

(1) That all these evils are from now on to be ascribed solely to a social order which no longer corresponds to the requirements of the real situation; and

(2) That it is possible, through a new social order, to do away with these evils altogether.

QUESTION 14. WHAT WILL THIS NEW SOCIAL ORDER
HAVE TO BE LIKE?

ANSWER. Above all, it will have to take the control of industry and of all branches of production out of the hands of mutually competing individuals, and instead institute a system in which all these branches of production are operated by society as a whole, that is, for the common account, according to a common plan, and with the participation of all members of society. It will, in other words, abolish competition and replace it with association. Moreover, since the management of industry by individuals necessarily implies private property, and since competition is in reality merely the manner and form in which the control of industry by private property owners expresses itself, it follows that private property cannot be separated from competition and the individual management of industry. Private property must therefore be abolished and in its place must come the common utilization of all instruments of production and the distribution of all products according to common agreement— in a word, what is called the communal ownership of goods. In fact, the abolition of private property is doubtless the shortest and most significant way to characterize the revolution in the whole social order which has been made necessary by the development of industry, and for this reason it is rightly advanced by communists as their main demand.

QUESTION 15. WAS NOT THE ABOLITION OF PRIVATE PROPERTY POSSIBLE AT AN EARLIER TIME?

ANSWER. No. Every change in the social order, every revolution in property relations, is the necessary consequence of the creation of new forces of production which no longer fit into the old property relations. Private property itself originated in this way. For private property has not always existed. When, towards the end of the Middle Ages, there arose a new mode of production which could not be carried on under the then existing feudal and guild forms of property, this manufacture, which had outgrown the old property relations, created a new property form, private property. And for manufacture and the earliest stage of development of big industry, private property was the only possible property form; the social order based on it was the only possible social order. So long as it is not possible to produce so much that there is enough for all, with more left over for expanding the social capital and extending the forces of production—so long as this is not possible, there must always be a ruling class directing the use of society's productive forces, and a poor, oppressed class. How these classes are constituted depends on the stage of development. The agrarian Middle Ages give us the baron and the serf; the cities of the later Middle Ages show us the guildmaster and the journeyman and the day laborer; the seventeenth century has its manufacturers and manufacturing workers; the nineteenth has big factory owners and proletarians. It is clear that up to now the forces of production have never been developed to the point where enough could be produced for all, and that private property has become a fetter and a barrier in relation to the further development of the forces of production. Now, however, the development of big industry has ushered in a new period. Capital and the forces of production have been expanded to an unprecedented extent, and the means are at hand to multiply them without limit in the near future. Moreover, the forces of production have been concentrated in the hands of a few bourgeois, while the great mass of the people are more and more falling into the proletariat, their situation becoming more wretched and intolerable in proportion to the increase of wealth of the bourgeoisie. And finally, these mighty and easily extended forces of production have so far outgrown private property and the bourgeoisie that they threaten at any moment to unleash the most violent disturbances of the social order. Now, under these conditions, the abolition of private property has become not only possible but absolutely necessary.

QUESTION 16. WILL THE PEACEFUL ABOLITION OF PRIVATE PROPERTY BE POSSIBLE?

ANSWER. It would be desirable if this could happen, and the communists would certainly be the last to oppose it. Communists know only too well that all conspiracies are not only useless but even harmful. They know all too well that revolutions are not made intentionally and arbitrarily, but that everywhere and always they have been the necessary consequence of conditions which were wholly independent of the will and direction of individual parties and entire classes. But they also see that the development of the proletariat in nearly all civilized countries has been violently suppressed, and that in this way the opponents of communism have been working toward a revolution with all their strength. If the oppressed proletariat is finally driven to revolution, then we communists will defend the interests of the proletarians with deeds as we now defend them with words.

QUESTION 17. WILL IT BE POSSIBLE FOR PRIVATE PROPERTY TO BE ABOLISHED AT ONE STROKE?

ANSWER. No, no more than existing forces of production can at one stroke be multiplied to the extent necessary for the creation of a communal society. In all probability, the proletarian revolution will transform existing society gradually and will be able to abolish private property only when the means of production are available in sufficient quantity.

QUESTION 18. WHAT WILL BE THE COURSE OF THIS REVOLUTION?

ANSWER. Above all, it will establish a *democratic constitution* and through this the direct or indirect dominance of the proletariat. Direct in England, where the proletarians are already a majority of the people. Indirect in France and Germany, where the majority of the people consists not only of proletarians but also of small peasants and petty bourgeois who are in the process of falling into the proletariat, who are more and more dependent in all their political interests on the proletariat, and who must therefore soon adapt themselves to the demands of the proletariat. Perhaps this will cost a second struggle, but the outcome can only be the victory of the proletariat.

Democracy would be wholly valueless to the proletariat if it were not immediately used as a means for putting through measures directed against private property and ensuring the livelihood of the proletariat. The main measures, emerging as the necessary result of existing relations, are the following:

(1) Limitations of private property through progressive taxation, heavy inheritance taxes, abolition of inheritance through collateral lines (brothers, nephews, etc.), forced loans, etc.

(2) Gradual expropriation of landowners, industrialists, railroad magnates and shipowners, partly through competition by state industry, partly directly through compensation in the form of bonds.

(3) Confiscation of the possessions of all emigrants and rebels against the majority of the people.

(4) Organization of labor or employment of proletarians on publicly owned land, in factories and workshops, with competition among the workers being abolished and with the factory owners, insofar as they still exist, being obliged to pay the same high wages as those paid by the state.

(5) An equal obligation on all members of society to work until such time as private property has been completely abolished. Formation of industrial armies, especially for agriculture.

(6) Centralization of money and credit in the hands of the state through a national bank operating with state capital, and the suppression of all private banks and bankers.

(7) Expansion of the number of national factories, workshops, railroads, ships; bringing new lands into cultivation and improvement of land already under cultivation—all in proportion to the growth of the capital and labor force at the disposal of the nation.

(8) Education of all children, from the moment they can leave their mothers' care, in national establishments at national cost. Education and production together.

(9) Construction, on public lands, of great palaces as communal dwellings for associated groups of citizens engaged in both industry and agriculture and combining in their way of life the advantages of urban and rural conditions while avoiding the one-sidedness and drawbacks of each.

(10) Destruction of all unhealthy and jerry-built dwellings in urban districts.

(11) Equal inheritance rights for children born in and out of wedlock.

(12) Concentration of all means of transportation in the hands of the nation.

It is impossible, of course, to carry out all these measures at once. But one will always bring others in its wake. Once the first radical attack on private property has been launched, the proletariat will find itself forced to go ever further, to concentrate increasingly in the hands of the state all capital, all agriculture, all transport, all trade. All the foregoing measures are directed to this end; and they will become practicable and feasible, capable of producing their centralizing effects to precisely the degree that the proletariat through its labor multiplies the country's productive forces. Finally, when all capital, all production, all exchange have been brought together in the hands of the nation, private property will disappear of its own accord, money will become superfluous, and production will so expand and man so change that society will be able to slough off whatever of its old economic habits may remain.

QUESTION 19. WILL IT BE POSSIBLE FOR THIS REVOLUTION TO TAKE PLACE IN ONE COUNTRY ALONE?

ANSWER. No. By creating the world market, big industry has already brought all the peoples of the earth, and especially the civilized peoples, into such close relation with one another that none is independent of what happens to the others. Further, it has coordinated the social development of the civilized countries to such an extent that in all of them bourgeoisie and proletariat have become the decisive classes and the struggle between them the great struggle of the day. It follows that the communist revolution will be not merely a national phenomenon but must take place simultaneously in all civilized countries, that is to say, at least in England, America, France, and Germany. It will develop in each of these countries more or less rapidly according as one country or the other has a more developed industry, greater wealth, a more significant mass of productive forces. Hence it will go slowest and will meet most obstacles in Germany, most rapidly and with the fewest difficulties in England. It will have a powerful impact on the other countries of the world and will radically alter the course of development which they have followed up to now, while greatly stepping up its pace. It is a universal revolution and will accordingly have a universal range.

QUESTION 20. WHAT WILL BE THE CONSEQUENCES OF THE ULTIMATE DISAPPEARANCE OF PRIVATE PROPERTY?

ANSWER. Society will take all forces of production and means of commerce, as well as the exchange and distribution of products, out of the hands of private capitalists and will manage them in accordance with a plan based on the availability of resources and the needs of the whole society. In this way, most important of all, the evil consequences which are now associated with the conduct of big industry will be abolished. There will be no more crises; the expanded production, which for the present order of society is overproduction and hence a prevailing cause of misery, will then be insufficient and in need of being expanded much further. Instead of generating misery, overproduction will reach beyond the elementary requirements of society to assure the satisfaction of the needs of all; it will create new needs and at the same time the means of satisfying them. It will become the condition of and the stimulus to new progress which will no longer throw the whole social order into confusion, as progress has always done in the past. Big industry, freed from the pressure of private property, will undergo such an expansion that what we now see will seem as petty in comparison as manufacture seems when put beside the big industry of our own day. This development of industry will make available to society a sufficient mass of products to satisfy the needs of everyone. The same will be true of agriculture, which also suffers from the pressure of private property and is held back by the division of privately owned land into small parcels. Here existing improvements and scientific procedures will be put into practice, with a resulting leap forward which will assure to society all the products it needs. In this way such an abundance of goods will be produced that society will be able to satisfy the needs of all its members. The division of society into different, mutually hostile classes will then become unnecessary. Indeed, it will be not only unnecessary but intolerable in the new social order. The existence of classes originated in the division of labor, and the division of labor as it has been known up to the present will completely disappear. For mechanical and chemical processes are not enough to bring industrial and agricultural production up to the level we have described; the capacities of the men who make use of these processes must undergo a corresponding development. Just as the peasants and manufacturing workers of the last century changed their whole way of life and became quite different people when they were impressed into big industry, in the same way communal control over production by society as a whole and the resulting new development will both require an entirely different kind of human material. People will no longer be, as they are today, subordinated to a single branch of production, bound to it, exploited by it; they will no longer develop one of their faculties at the expense of all others; they will no longer know only one branch, or one branch of a single branch, of production as a whole. Even industry as it is today is finding such people less and less useful. Industry controlled by society as a whole and operated according to a plan presupposes well-rounded human beings, their faculties developed in balanced fashion, able to see the system of production in its entirety. The form of the division of labor which makes one a peasant, another a cobbler, a third a factory worker, a fourth a stock-market operator has already been undermined by machinery and will completely disappear. Education will enable young people quickly to familiarize themselves with the whole system of production and to pass from one branch of production to another in response to the needs of society or their own inclinations. It will therefore free them from the one-sided character which the present-day division of labor impresses upon every individual. Communist society will in this way make it possible for its members to put their comprehensively developed faculties to full use. But when this happens classes will necessarily disappear. It follows that society organized on a communist basis is incompatible with the existence of classes on the one hand, and that the very building of such a society provides the means of abolishing class differences on the other.

A corollary of this is that the difference between city and country is destined to disappear. The management of agriculture and industry by the same people rather than by two different classes of people is, if only for purely material reasons, a necessary condition of communist association. The dispersal of the agricultural population on the land alongside the crowding of the industrial population into the great cities is a condition which corresponds to an undeveloped state of both agriculture and industry and can already be felt as an obstacle to further development.

The general cooperation of all members of society for the purpose of planned exploitation of the forces of production, the expansion of production to the point where it will satisfy the needs of all, the abolition of a situation in which the needs of some are satisfied at the expense of the needs of others, the complete liquidation of classes and their conflicts, the rounded development of the capacities of all members of society through the elimination of the present division of labor, through the participation by all in the enjoyments produced by all, through the combination of city and country— these are the main consequences of the abolition of private property.

QUESTION 21. WHAT WILL BE THE INFLUENCE OF COMMUNIST SOCIETY ON THE FAMILY?

ANSWER. It will transform the relations between the sexes into a purely private matter which concerns only the persons involved and into which society has no occasion to intervene. It can do this since it does away with private property and educates children on a communal basis, and in this way removes the two bases of traditional marriage, the dependence, rooted in private property, of the woman on the man and the children on the parents. And here is the answer to the outcry of the highly moral philistines against the "community of women." Community of women is a condition which belongs entirely to bourgeois society and which today finds its complete expression in prostitution. But prostitution is based on private property and falls with it. Thus communist society, instead of introducing community of women, in fact abolishes it.

QUESTION 22. WHAT WILL BE THE ATTITUDE OF COMMUNISM TO EXISTING NATIONALITIES?

ANSWER. As is.[1]

QUESTION 23. WHAT WILL BE ITS ATTITUDE TO EXISTING RELIGIONS?

ANSWER. As is.[1]

---

[1] The editor of the Marx-Engels *Gesamtausgabe* surmises that this is a reference to an earlier draft which had been prepared by Engels's comrades in Paris. He definitely rejects the explanation put forward by Eduard Bernstein when he first published the Engels manuscript, that the reference is to an earlier draft prepared by Engels himself. —Paul M. Sweezy

QUESTION 24. HOW DO COMMUNISTS DIFFER FROM SOCIALISTS?

ANSWER. The so-called socialists are divided into three categories.

The first category consists of adherents of a feudal and patriarchal society which has already been destroyed, and is still daily being destroyed, by big industry and world trade and their creation, bourgeois society. This category concludes from the evils of existing society that feudal and patriarchal society must be restored because it was free of such evils. In one way or another all their proposals are directed to this end. This category of *reactionary* socialists, for all their seeming partisanship and their scalding tears for the misery of the proletariat, is nevertheless energetically opposed by the communists for the following reasons:

(1) It strives for something which is entirely impossible.

(2) It seeks to establish the rule of the aristocracy, the guild-masters, the small producers, and their retinue of absolute or feudal monarchs, officials, soldiers, and priests—a society which was, to be sure, free of the evils of present-day society but which brought with it at least as many evils without even offering to the oppressed workers the prospect of liberation through a communist revolution.

(3) As soon as the proletariat becomes revolutionary and communist, these reactionary socialists show their true colors by immediately making common cause with the bourgeoisie against the proletarians.

The second category consists of adherents of present-day society who have been frightened for its future by the evils to which it necessarily gives rise. What they want, therefore, is to maintain this society while getting rid of the evils which are an inherent part of it. To this end, some propose mere welfare measures while others come forward with grandiose systems of reform which under the pretense of reorganizing society are in fact intended to preserve the foundations, and hence the life, of existing society.

Communists must unremittingly struggle against these *bourgeois socialists* because they work for the enemies of communists and protect the society which communists aim to overthrow.

Finally, the third category consists of democratic socialists who favor some of the same measures the communists advocate, as described by Question 18, not as part of the transition to communism, however, but rather as measures which they believe will be sufficient to abolish the misery and the evils of present-day society. These *democratic socialists* are either proletarians who are not yet sufficiently clear about the conditions of the liberation of their class, or they are representatives of the petty bourgeoisie, a class which, prior to the achievement of democracy and the socialist measures to which it gives rise, has many interests in common with the proletariat. It follows that in moments of action the communists will have to come to an understanding with these democratic socialists, and in general to follow as far as possible a common policy with them, provided that these socialists do not enter into the service of the ruling bourgeoisie and attack the communists. It is clear that this form of cooperation in action does not exclude the discussion of differences.

QUESTION 25. WHAT IS THE ATTITUDE OF THE COMMUNISTS TO THE OTHER POLITICAL PARTIES OF OUR TIME?

ANSWER. This attitude is different in the different countries.

In England, France, and Belgium, where the bourgeoisie rules, the communists still have a common interest with the various democratic parties, an interest which is all the greater the more closely the socialistic measures they champion approach the aims of the communists, that is, the more clearly and definitely they represent the interests of the proletariat and the more they depend on the proletariat for support. In England, for example, the working-class Chartists are infinitely closer to the communists than the democratic petty bourgeoisie or the so-called Radicals.

In America, where a democratic constitution has already been established, the communists must take common cause with the part which will turn this constitution against the bourgeoisie and use it in the interests of the proletariat, that is, with the agrarian National Reformers.[2]

In Switzerland, the Radicals, though a very mixed party, are the only group with which the communists can cooperate, and among these Radicals the Vaudois and Genevese are the most advanced.

In Germany, finally, the decisive struggle now on the order of the day is that between the bourgeoisie and the absolute monarchy. Since the communists cannot enter upon the decisive struggle between themselves and the bourgeoisie until the bourgeoisie is in power, it follows that it is to the interest of the communists to help the bourgeoisie to power as soon as possible in order the sooner to be able to overthrow it. Against the governments, therefore, the communists must continually support the radical liberal party, taking care to avoid the self-deceptions of the bourgeoisie and not to fall for the enticing promises of benefits which a victory for the bourgeoisie would allegedly bring to the proletariat. The sole advantages which the proletariat would derive from a bourgeois victory would consist (1) in various concessions which would facilitate the tasks of the communists in guarding, discussing, and propagating their principles and would hence also facilitate the unification of the proletariat into a closely knit, battle-worthy, and organized class; and (2) in the certainty that on the very day the absolute monarchies fall, the struggle between bourgeoisie and proletariat will start. From that day on, the policy of the communists will be the same as it now is in the countries where the bourgeoisie is already in power.

---

[2] Probably a reference to the National Reform Association, founded during the 1840s by George H. Evans, a movement with headquarters in New York City which had for its motto "Vote Yourself a Farm."—Paul M. Sweezy

THE
COMMUNIST MANIFESTO
150 YEARS LATER

Ellen Meiksins Wood

THE COMMUNIST MANIFESTO
150 YEARS LATER

The *Communist Manifesto* is just that: a manifesto. It is not a long and comprehensive scholarly study but a public declaration of a political program, a short and dramatic statement of purpose and a call to arms, written at a time of political ferment, on the eve of what turned out to be the nearest thing the world had ever seen to international revolution.

Yet posterity has judged this political manifesto not just as a manifesto but as many other things. In the century and a half since its publication, it has been judged not only as a uniquely influential document in the theory and practice of revolutionary movements throughout the world, but also as a work of history, as economic, political, and cultural analysis, and as prophecy. The *Manifesto* has been judged as an account of past, present, and future—not only the present and future of its authors but those of every generation since, up to and including our own.

At first glance, it seems very unreasonable to judge a small pamphlet—the product of collaboration by two young men very early in their careers, written for a very specific and immediate purpose—by such demanding measures. It is hard to think of any other classic of Western social thought that has been judged by such sweeping and rigorous standards. The *Manifesto* stands alone in this respect no doubt because of its tremendous role in the history of a vast political movement which has had an immeasurable influence on the shape of the modern world. More particularly, the *Manifesto* has been subject to uniquely critical scrutiny because people in power, and their intellectual supporters, have felt that much was at stake in debunking it.

But only a very great work—which still has much to say to us 150 years later—could invite this kind of critical scrutiny. Nothing could give more convincing testimony to the genius of the *Manifesto* than the energy that has been expended in attacking it. So while we have to remember the particular purposes for which it was written and the very specific historical context in which it emerged, it seems not so unreasonable after all to judge it in much larger terms.

The Historical Context of the Manifesto

Let us first consider the context in which the *Communist Manifesto* was written and how the specific historical conditions of its composition affected its content.

The broad historical context of the *Manifesto* is, of course, the emergence of industrial capitalism and the modern industrial working class in Western Europe, together with the socialist movements that grew out of these historical developments. There had been earlier classics in what would become the socialist tradition—such as the work of Winstanley in seventeenth century England or Babeuf in eighteenth century France—but the social movements with which they were associated, while influential in various ways, remained on the margins of history. It was only in the nineteenth century that substantial working class movements emerged that could form a powerful political force and even socialist parties. With the appearance of this new political force came a body of socialist literature. First, there was a diverse collection of writings often treated together (largely thanks to the *Manifesto* itself) under the category "utopian socialism," by thinkers such as Owen, St. Simon, and Fourier. These writings would be overtaken by the far more penetrating and systematic works of Marx and Engels, whose socialism was deeply rooted in a critical analysis of capitalism of a kind never attempted before. The *Manifesto* is certainly not the most substantial of these works, but it is without doubt the most well known, with a historical resonance probably unsurpassed by any other single piece of secular writing, from any part of the political spectrum.

Yet though the *Manifesto* was composed against the background of those larger, long-term historical developments, it had a more immediate context which helps to explain its particular shape. The pamphlet was commissioned by the German Communist League in 1847. Friedrich Engels (at age 27) first drafted *Principles of Communism* (also included in this edition). He handed it over to Karl Marx, then 29, for revision. Drawing on Engels' *Principles*, Marx produced the theoretical and literary masterpiece we now know as the *Communist Manifesto*, which was first published anonymously in London in February 1848.

This was the year when revolution would sweep across Europe—almost immediately after the publication of the *Manifesto* (though obviously not because of it). Spreading like wildfire from France to Germany to Hungary, Italy, and beyond, the revolution covered an area that today takes in at least part of ten different European countries, with effects as far away as Latin America. In just a few weeks, one government after another fell. These revolutions were to be very short-lived, but it is hard to over-estimate the hopes and fears they aroused as signals of an international revolution.

The *Manifesto* was written just before the outbreak of the revolution. Although it cannot be said that the pamphlet played a major part in the events that followed, it is a product of that very specific time and that very specific revolutionary climate. In that historical fact lies both many of its strengths and some unresolved problems.

The revolution, or revolutions, of 1848 took place in countries with very diverse social, economic, and political conditions: from a relatively "developed" country like France, or parts of Germany (not yet a single unified state) such as the Rhineland, to "backward" areas like southern Italy or Transylvania. But one thing they had in common was that capitalism was not well advanced in any of them, and in some cases not at all. For all their differences, too, they all had predominantly rural populations. Britain, the country in which capitalism was most advanced, certainly saw eruptions of popular unrest and state repression in the 1840s, but it did not experience the revolutionary upheavals that occurred on the Continent. There was a mass political movement in Britain too, the Chartist movement, but its political struggles (for instance, the struggle for an extension of the franchise to the working class, which would be won some time later) were being overtaken by new kinds of class struggle. The growth of industrial capitalism was already shifting the central terrain of class conflict from the political arena to the workplace, the "point of production."

If the various Continental revolutions had a common political program, it was not the overthrow of something like a capitalist system. It was rather the establishment of unified liberal or constitutional states with a degree of civil equality, inspired above all by the French Revolution in the previous century. In some cases, like Hungary or Italy, the struggle for a more democratic state was bound up with the fight for national autonomy.

But if 1848 was not a socialist or anti-capitalist revolution, neither was it unambiguously a "bourgeois revolution" in the now commonly understood sense: a revolution to liberate capitalism from feudal constraints. The revolutionary "bourgeoisie" was not a coherent capitalist class. Prominent among them were civil servants, professionals, and intellectuals. Even in countries where industrialization was more advanced, the industrial bourgeoisie which opposed the dominant regime was small and relatively weak, never able to act alone against the ruling elite without the support of popular forces with different material interests.

In all these cases, too, the popular forces, the people who fought and died in the streets, the people who pushed the revolution beyond the political objectives of the "bourgeois republic" or the liberal state toward more far-reaching social transformations, were not a modern mass proletariat. They included independent craftsmen, small shop-keepers, in some places peasants (like Italy, and even some parts of Germany), and the unemployed or underemployed poor in towns with undeveloped economies still unable to absorb them. Nowhere in revolutionary Europe was there a massive and developed proletariat, a sizeable class of wage-laborers employed by capital such as already existed in Britain. The nascent proletariat, especially in France and more devel-oped parts of Germany, had an effect disproportionate to its numbers, but it could not yet provide the social base for a successful revolution.

For that matter, there may have been no solid social base even for a "bourgeois democratic" revolution. The revolutionary movements relied, to varying degrees, on mass mobilization. Yet it was precisely the dangers of mass mobilization that quickly drove bourgeois liberals and radicals everywhere away from democracy, or even liberalism, and back to rigid hierarchy, order, and reaction. It might be said that the revolution both erupted and failed because no single class was strong enough to sustain a stable regime of its own.

At any rate, when Marx and Engels wrote the *Manifesto*, they did not believe that a socialist revolution, or a proletarian revolution of any kind, was in the offing. They briefly hoped that the events, and the failures, of 1848 might lead to something more, some further longer-term development, a "permanent revolution" that would push beyond the bourgeois republic to proletarian rule and finally socialism. But any reader of the *Manifesto* must be struck by the fact that the revolutionary hero of its eloquent narrative is the bourgeoisie.

The revolutionary victories of the bourgeoisie were, of course, deeply contradictory for Marx and Engels, combining benefits and costs in equal measure. They hoped, and confidently expected, that the bourgeoisie's conquests would eventually be overtaken by the triumph of the working class and socialism. But even while the *Manifesto* calls workers to arms and foresees their emergence as a truly revolutionary force, it tells the triumphal story of the bourgeoisie.

It is commonly acknowledged that the "bourgeois revolution," with the French Revolution of 1789 as the guiding light, forms the background of the *Communist Manifesto*. But what exactly does this mean, and what are its consequences for the argument of the *Manifesto*?

We cannot make sense of this classic without understanding that the setting of its historical narrative is not an advanced capitalism. The point is not simply that the pamphlet was written in the mid-nineteenth century rather than at the end of the twentieth. It is not just that Marx and Engels were talking about an earlier stage of capitalism than the one we inhabit. The immediate context of their narrative is not even the most advanced capitalism of their own day. They are writing against the background of revolutionary ferment generated by social forces and struggles that have as much to do with pre-capitalist formations as with capitalist social relations: not just wage-laborers pitted against capitalist employers, but non-privileged against privileged classes, common people (including bourgeois) against aristocracy, the nation against monarchy, peasants against landlords, even serfs against masters, and everywhere the hungry poor against the rich.

This is where we come to some interesting tensions in the *Manifesto*. It is a manifesto of communism, of proletarian revolution against capitalism. As a call to socialist struggle, it has never been surpassed in its passion, its eloquence, its depth. It is also a powerful and prophetic analysis of capitalism, which still stands unrivalled as a portrait of the capitalist world in which we live today, even on the brink of the twenty-first century. But the *Manifesto*'s immediate political inspiration belongs to a different world, very unlike the capitalist world it so vividly portrays.

Marx's projections of the capitalist future are remarkable enough even in relation to the most advanced capitalism of his day. But if Britain was the model for his analysis of the capitalist system, it was not the inspiration for the *Manifesto*'s story of the bourgeoisie as a revolutionary*political* force—a force that would, in turn, launch the career of the proletariat as a revolutionary class.

The narrative of bourgeois revolution portrays the bourgeoisie as a class which, at every stage of its development, was obliged to struggle against the forces of reaction. It began, says Marx, as an oppressed class fighting against the feudal aristocracy and, only after centuries of class struggle and advance, ended with its own modern representative state. In all these battles it was obliged to enlist the support of laboring classes, and finally to drag the modern proletariat into the political arena, giving the working class the weapons to conduct its own struggle against the bourgeoisie. This bourgeoisie also bequeathed to the working class the most progressive aspects of its ideology: critical, anti-clerical and anti-superstitious, liberal and up to a point egalitarian—in other words, the culture of the Enlightenment.

This portrait of a politically progressive bourgeoisie, anti-aristocratic to its core and more or less liberal, owes more to the history of Continental bourgeois struggles than to the development of British capitalism. The classic "bourgeois" struggle, the French Revolution of 1789, had little to do with capitalism. The core of the revolutionary bourgeoisie did not consist of capitalists, or even of commercial classes of a pre-capitalist kind, but of office-holders and professionals. The revolutionary objectives of people like this had to do not with liberating capitalism but with aspirations to civil equality and "careers open to talent." These bourgeois objectives are not those of a society in which capitalist wealth is the highest goal. They were better suited to a society in which public office was a lucrative economic resource and the highest bourgeois career.

As for British *capitalism*, it was never simply, or even primarily, a "bourgeois" career. The British landed aristocracy was no less capitalist than were urban classes. Nor did capitalism establish itself in England by means of politically progressive "bourgeois" struggles against a reactionary aristocracy. Many large property owners in England, both landed and urban, had certainly fought against the king in the English revolution of the seventeenth century, when their partnership with the

Crown threatened to give way to an "absolutist" monarchy; and they were obliged to resort to popular mobilization to achieve their anti-absolutist goals. In that struggle, they espoused certain principles of parliamentary rule and "limited" government, and the popular forces they unleashed (and soon suppressed) produced some of the most radically democratic ideas the world had ever seen. But the revolution was never a class struggle between a landed aristocracy and a rising bourgeoisie, capitalist or otherwise.

If capitalists in Britain were ever compelled to engage in class struggle to ensure their own class interests, it was not a struggle against a ruling class. In a sense, capitalists—at least agrarian capitalists—were *born* a ruling class in England. Even in the nineteenth century, when conflicts erupted between landed and industrial classes, they were essentially conflicts between two kinds of capital. If British capitalism required class struggle to free itself from political and economic constraints, it was primarily against subordinate classes, such as the small proprietors whose property rights (and sometimes dangerously radical ideas) interfered with capitalist accumulation.

So it was not really capitalists who supplied Marx with his principal model of a politically progressive bourgeoisie. Yet that progressive model did affect his view of capitalism. It is difficult to say how much his hopes for proletarian revolution were encouraged by this image of a politically progressive bourgeoisie which launched the proletariat onto the political stage and furthered its political development. But one thing seems clear: the picture of capitalism itself as a progressive force—which is so much a part of the *Manifesto*'s story—is colored by the revolutionary career of the Continental, and especially the French, bourgeoisie.

We have to draw some distinctions in the *Manifesto* between the story of political, cultural, and ideological progress, on the one hand, and the analysis of material or economic development, on the other. Or, more precisely, we have to distinguish between those political, cultural, and ideological developments that are clearly associated with capitalist economic development and those that are not so clearly connected with capitalism. The different aspects of Marx's narrative, conflated in his own account, are typically lumped together by commentators, often under the general heading of "modernity." But it will make for a better understanding of capitalism if we try to disentangle some of the different strands in his narrative. This will bring out in sharper relief Marx's own remarkable, and to this day unrivalled, insights into the nature of capitalism.

It is not at all clear that the development of capitalism required, or brought into being, the best of Enlightenment principles. For instance, that part of the French bourgeoisie which in the eighteenth century adopted as its guiding ideology the Enlightenment commitment to human improvement, the improvement of the human mind, the eradication of ignorance and superstition, or the commitment to civil equality and "careers open to talent," was not in the main a capitalist class. It was a class of professionals, office-holders, and intellectuals, with material interests distinct from those of capitalists. It can even be argued that the mature development of capitalism has brought an end to that kind of bourgeoisie and its specific cultural formation.

In the twentieth century we know all too well that capitalism, while it certainly requires a "rational" (that is, an "efficient" or profitable) organization of production, has little need for "rationalism" in the best Enlightenment sense: the submission of all authority to the scrutiny of critical reason. Capitalism needs a disciplined and docile workforce. It has no need at all for a critical citizenry. In fact, a worker who has a habit of using her critical reason may be much more dangerous to the "rational" organization of production (not to mention the power and property of capital) than would, say, a worker committed to some irrationalist superstition or certain kinds of religious fundamentalism which repudiate Enlightenment principles. Right-wing political movements in the U.S., for instance, have without any difficulty combined anti-Enlightenment values with a deep commitment to capitalism.

As for political progress, it is certainly true that feudal hierarchy and aristocratic privilege did, as Marx suggests, give way to the "modern representative state." In fact, since Marx wrote those words the "bourgeois" representative state has itself given way to something we now call "democracy." The bourgeoisie is not now a "ruling" class in the literal sense: its class dominance does not depend on exclusive access to political rights or on a clear and legally defined division between capitalist rulers and proletarian subjects. Workers are citizens with full voting rights, and capitalism has proved itself able to tolerate universal adult suffrage in a way that no other form of class domination has ever been able to do.

But this political advance has been deeply ambiguous. The ambiguity goes beyond the obvious fact that in capitalist "democracy" wealth still means privileged access to political power, or the fact that the state, as Marx and Engels maintained, generally acts in the interests of the capitalist class. Nor is it just that capitalism can readily tolerate, and sometimes needs, authoritarian rule. There is an even more fundamental contradiction in capitalist "democracy."

Capitalism can tolerate "democracy" because capitalists control the labor of others not by means of exclusive political rights but by means of exclusive property. Although capital needs the support of the state, workers are compelled to sell their labor power for purely "economic" reasons. Since they do not own the means of production, the sale of labor power for a wage is the only way they can gain access to the conditions of subsistence, and even to the means of their own labor. There is no immediate need for direct political coercion to make them work for capital. Purely "economic" compulsions are generally enough.

This means that even in its best and most "democratic" forms, capitalism can, and must, confine equality to a separate "political" sphere which does not, and must not, intrude into the economic sphere or subvert economic inequality. A kind of democracy may prevail in the political sphere, but people in capitalist societies spend most of their waking lives in activities and relationships where there is no democratic accountability at all. This is true not only in the workplace, where they are likely to be under the direct control of others, but in all spheres of life that are subject to "market" imperatives.

So capitalism has created a political sphere governed by "democracy," but it has at the same time, and by the same means, put large areas of human life outside the reach of democracy. In other words, much of what capitalism has given with one hand it has taken away with the other.

Marx's analysis of capitalism is so rich precisely because it exposes the system's fundamental contradictions. The tendency to conflate "bourgeois" and "capitalist," and to tell their stories as a single story of "modernity" and progress, can obscure those contradictions. It may detract from those aspects of Marx's analysis which give us an insight, sharper and deeper than ever before or since, into the nature of capitalist society. In his later work, and especially in *Capital*, Marx would provide a much more exhaustive analysis of capitalism. But in the few pages devoted to it in the *Manifesto*, in poetic and passionate prose yet with stark and penetrating clarity, he captures, as no one else has ever done, the essence of capitalism, with all its dynamism and destructiveness.

Capitalism and Historical Materialism

The bourgeoisie cannot exist without constantly revolutionizing the instruments of production, and thereby the relations of production, and with them the whole relations of society. Conservation of the old modes of production in unaltered form was, on the contrary, the first condition of existence for all earlier industrial classes. Constant revolutionizing of production, uninterrupted disturbances of all social conditions, everlasting uncertainty and agitation distinguish the bourgeois era from all earlier ones. All fixed, fast-frozen relations...are swept away, all new-formed ones become antiquated before they can ossify. All that is solid melts into air, all that is holy is profaned....

In this, one of the most famous passages in the *Manifesto*, Marx sums up the nature of capitalism. Unlike all other earlier social forms, capitalism demands constant change, constant improvement of productive forces to enhance the productivity of labor in a constant quest for profit. The need for profit, the need to accumulate endlessly, is imposed on capital by the very nature of the system: it *must* accumulate, it *must* maximize profit, just to survive. No earlier system was ever subject to such pressures.

This characterization of capitalism as a specific mode of production different from others is based on the principles of historical materialism, which Marx and Engels had been elaborating for several years and which they would develop more fully after 1848. Historical materialism begins with the simple proposition that human beings obtain the material conditions of their existence through specific and historically variable relationships with nature and with other human beings. The most basic fact about any form of social organization is the nature of those relationships, the specific ways in which any given society goes about providing the material conditions of existence.

There came a point in human history when the social organization of material life took the form of class divisions, the divisions between people who labored and those who exploited the labor of others. That division inevitably led to conflict, and since then history, the *Manifesto* proclaims, has been propelled by those class struggles, as exploited classes have resisted exploitation. But while class struggle has been a moving force of history since the beginning of class society, it has taken different forms in different societies. Each particular mode of production, each system of class relations, has its own internal logic, its own requirements, its own conditions of survival and success, its own dynamics, its own forms of conflict and struggle. And capitalism has very specific conditions that, unlike any previous mode of production, demand the constant revolutionizing of productive forces.

In *Principles of Communism*, Engels suggests that history from the beginning has been moved forward by the constant progress of productive forces, especially technological improvement, and that social relations have been compelled to adapt to these developing forces. This conception of technological progress, which owes much to the Enlightenment and to classical political economy, appears in the *Manifesto* too.

But in Marx's version, the emphasis is less on some transhistorical process of technological progress and more on the historically specific effects of particular social relations. His emphasis is above all on the ways in which the distinctive conditions of capitalism, the relationship between an exploiting class of capitalists and a propertyless class of wage laborers, has been accompanied by a historically *unique* drive to revolutionize productive forces. Throughout history, there has certainly been a long-term improvement of productive forces; but, as Marx tells us, all societies before capitalism had a built-in tendency to keep production as it was. Only capitalism has broken that universal rule and created new pressures constantly to enhance labor productivity by technical means.

The pressure to accumulate and to revolutionize the instruments of production is rooted in the capitalist mode of exploitation, the means by which capital extracts labor from workers. Capitalists are dependent on the market both to acquire the means of producing goods or services and to sell those goods or services. Even the labor-power of workers is a commodity, which capitalists buy for a fixed period of time in exchange for a wage. Capital then puts that labor-power to work and seeks to obtain the maximum output in limited time at minimum cost. So capital is constantly seeking new techniques, new instruments, new modes of organization and control, to increase the productivity of labor, in order to meet competition in the market. To produce "competitively" for the market inevitably means constant accumulation and profit-maximization. It also means constant change: new technologies, new commodities, new services, new needs, new forms of organization, and new social arrangements.

Marx emphasizes the historical uniqueness of a system in which the provision of virtually all human needs and wants is organized in this unprecedented way, where everything, even the most basic requirements like food and shelter, is produced for a profit. The effects of such a system on human life and social relations, not to mention nature itself, are bound to be drastic and far-reaching. In a few short passages, Marx dramatically conveys the consequences of a system in which everything—not only things, but nature and human activity—becomes a commodity to buy and sell on the market, and where human relations are reduced to "callous cash payment."

On the eve of the twenty-first century, when the commodification of life has gone so far that it is hard to imagine how it could go any further, when everything from food to culture to health care is distorted by market imperatives, we know all too well what this means. We know how destructive these market imperatives can be to the social fabric and the natural environment. We know their costs in poverty, in crime, in environmental pollution, in the waste of natural resources and human lives. Yet in Marx's day the process of commodification was far less advanced, and his prescience is truly remarkable.

Remarkable, too, is his insight into the effects of this system on labor. The exploitation of workers, their compulsion to work not only to sustain themselves and their families but to create maximum profits for their employers, is the essence of the story. But there is also the question of what happens to human labor when it is transformed from the exercise of human creativity into just a profit-making activity, or a commodity, whose value lies not in the satisfaction it gives to the worker or in its benefits to the community but in the gains it can realize in the market and in its contribution to capital accumulation.

It should be obvious that work is bound to be organized, and experienced, in different ways according to its purpose. The need to extract maximum output at minimum cost imposes very particular requirements, which inevitably have significant effects on human well-being. Marx describes the degradation of work when it is organized for the sole purpose of maximizing profit for the capitalist owners of the means of production. The effects are most visible where workers become mere "appendages" of the machine in an assembly line, but similar effects occur wherever the maximization of profit is the main motivation in the organization of work. What ought to be a creative and fulfilling activity is more likely to become just meaningless drudgery.

Yet capitalism also has, from Marx's point of view, some positive effects. The bourgeoisie, he says, "has accomplished wonders far surpassing Egyptian pyramids, Roman aqueducts, and Gothic cathedrals." It has "created more massive and more colossal productive forces than have all preceding generations together." Its revolutionizing of productive forces has created an unprecedented capacity to produce the material conditions of well-being for everyone.

But here is another paradox: if capitalism has created unprecedented material wealth, the capacity to maximize material well-being for everyone remains *only* a capacity, not a reality. Capitalism, indeed, *prevents* it from becoming a reality. One of the most fundamental contradictions of the capitalist system is the huge disparity between its "colossal" productive capacity and the quality of life it delivers.

One obvious sense in which this is true is that capitalist development has been inseparable from imperialisms of various kinds, from traditional forms of colonial exploitation to the current burden of debt in the third world, or the exploitation of cheap third world labor by today's "transnational" companies. The contradiction between capitalism's productive capacity and the quality of life is manifest today in the growing polarization between an opulent North and an indigent South. But the same contradiction is evident within the advanced capitalist economies themselves.

In a system where all production is for profit, the allocation of resources and labor will, of course, be determined not by their contribution to the well-being of as many people as possible but by their contribution to profitability. The society's productive capacities are much more likely to be devoted to producing, say, new model cars every year for those who can afford them, or computers designed to be obsolete as soon as they hit the market, than to providing decent affordable housing for all. So Marx would not be surprised that a society like the U.S., with the capacity to feed, clothe, house, educate, and provide health care for all its members, nevertheless has widespread poverty, homelessness, malnutrition, health care costs that many people cannot afford, and a system of education that leaves many functionally illiterate. Nor is it surprising that, in a society with such built-in inequities, there are deep social divisions, in which, for example, class exploitation and racism reinforce one another.

Still, capitalism has produced the *capacity* to maximize material well-being, and in that sense, it has laid a foundation for a different kind of society. Socialism would build on the productive forces created by capitalism, but it would eliminate the pressures for profit-maximization and capital accumulation which cause the disparity between productive capacity and the quality of life.

Capitalism has also, the *Manifesto* argues, created a social force, a class, with the capacity to overthrow capitalism and put socialism in its place. By giving birth to a mass proletariat, Marx maintains, capitalism has brought into being its own gravediggers. But many commentators, even on the socialist left, would now probably regard this as the most questionable assumption in the whole pamphlet. It is certainly true that capitalism has created a mass working class, both "blue collar" and "white collar" workers of various kinds who have in common their exploitation by capital. These workers are strategically situated at the heart of a system which depends on their labor, and that strategic location gives them a social power that could, as no other social force can, transform capitalism into socialism. It is also true that working class movements have fought many historic battles, won many important victories, and acted as a revolutionary force in many parts of the world. But, while Western Europe and North America have seen many episodes of mass working class radicalism, and some Western European countries may even have been brought to the brink of revolution, the working class has never yet brought about socialism in the advanced capitalist countries that seemed to Marx and Engels the most likely candidates. The result has been that even many socialists have become skeptical about the prospects for a new society.

We cannot assume that Marx's own optimism about the political development of the working class was quite as unalloyed as it seems in the *Manifesto*. He certainly knew that there were forces dividing as well as uniting the working class, and that much organizational and educational effort would be required to turn the working class into an effective political force. But it was clearly not his intention in a political manifesto to dwell on the obstacles, and the picture is obviously a great deal more complicated than the one he paints in his rousing call to arms.

The prediction that the organization of production in industrial capitalism, together with improvements in transportation and communication, would increasingly unite the working class into a cohesive force has come true in some respects. And no one can deny that working class struggles have achieved major gains which have improved the quality of life for everyone, gains we now take for granted such as a shorter working day and unemployment insurance. But unifying tendencies have also been counteracted, and for the time being overcome, by other forces that *fragment* the working class. Workers are divided by race, gender, and many other "identities," not to mention by the resurgent nationalisms which have defied Marx's conviction that the global economy created by capitalism would be followed by a new kind of internationalism.

These are not the only factors that divide the working class. Paradoxically, it tends to be fragmented by the very organization of production in capitalism. Capitalist production tends to focus the grievances and struggles of workers on their individual workplaces and against their own particular employers. When Marx suggests that "every class struggle is a political struggle," he undoubtedly means that every class struggle, even in the workplace, and even over purely "economic" issues, is about class power and resistance to domination. But what this proposition does not say is that capitalism has created a distinctive kind of relation between the "economic" and the "political." Capitalism has in a sense *separated* "economic" from political struggles, simply because the "economy" now has a life, and a power structure, of its own. The capitalist market has its own "economic" imperatives; the capitalist workplace has its own hierarchies, authorities, and rules; and the dominant class, unlike any class before it, has economic powers that do not depend directly on political power, even though it ultimately depends on the state to sustain the system of property on which its class power rests. So workers may be, and often have been, very militant in their industrial conflicts with capital without their class struggles spilling over into the political sphere.

The *Manifesto*'s optimism about the coming of socialism has, of course, been contradicted by another, truly spectacular, development: the end, in the 1980s and 1990s, of the system brought into being in the decades following the Russian Revolution of 1917. It is true that the revolution was far from the ideal test of Marx's predictions. Russia was not an advanced industrial capitalism with a mass proletariat, the kind of society that Marx regarded as the right foundation for a socialist transformation. At the time of the revolution, there were certainly pockets of fairly advanced industry and, at least in the principal large cities, a very militant industrial proletariat. At the same time, Russia remained a largely peasant country, and many industrial workers themselves remained rooted in their peasant villages. In these and other ways, the Russian heartland itself would not have met Marx's criteria for an advanced capitalist society—even by the standards of his mid-nineteenth century model, Britain; and if we add what might be called the "third world" regions of the czarist empire, this massive country could hardly be said to meet Marx's prerequisites for a transition from capitalism to socialism.

At any rate, what eventually emerged in the Soviet Union was very different from the democratic society Marx envisaged when he talked about a socialism based on the "free association of direct producers." In fact, it should be emphasized that much of what has gone under the name of Communism in the twentieth century has had little to do with what the *Communist Manifesto* meant by the term or with the Communist movement to which Marx and Engels belonged. Even when Marx began to expect some kind of revolution in Russia, he always assumed that a truly *socialist* revolution would have to take place in a capitalist country with more advanced productive forces and a more developed proletariat, a country like Britain or the U.S. Only in tandem with a proletarian revolution in such an advanced capitalist country could a Russian Revolution become a transition to socialism. He seems to have assumed that only well developed productive forces and a mature mass proletariat could direct production toward the fulfillment of the whole community's needs—not for capitalist profit nor for the benefit of any other kind of ruling class, and not controlled from above by an authoritarian state but under the democratic control of the "freely associated direct producers," the workers themselves.

Capitalism had taken centuries to create a mass proletariat and to accomplish even the development of productive forces available in Marx's day. It had done these things with many oppressions, atrocities, and tragedies along the way. Marx never sought, nor has anyone else yet found, a democratic, socialist way of achieving that kind of development. He regarded this contradictory achievement not as the task of socialism but as its precondition.

This is not to deny that the Soviet Union did, in fact, succeed in developing productive forces far beyond what Marx could have foreseen, and with exceptional speed. The point is rather that it would have been very difficult to accomplish such intensive development by means of the democratic organization of production that for Marx was the essence of socialism. To attain that level of development required a process of accumulation which capitalism had accomplished, over several centuries, not by democratic means but by expropriating small proprietors and by exploiting workers to the limits of their physical endurance. It would not have been easy to devise a democratic means of achieving comparable results. A truly democratic socialist party, a party very different from the oppressive Stalinist regime, would certainly have avoided the monstrosities of Stalinism. But even the most democratic socialist party, if obliged to administer the process of accumulation and to enforce the kind of intensive labor this required, would have found itself in a very difficult and contradictory relationship with the working class it was supposed to represent.

No one would claim that Marx foresaw what might happen if a revolution in the name of communism did take place in a less developed country. It is even less likely that he could have foreseen the crimes perpetrated by Stalinism in the name of communism. But we should not underestimate the significance of his assumption that a socialist revolution would be most likely to succeed in the context of a more advanced capitalism. In that sense, it could be argued that the ultimate failure of the Russian Revolution, which occurred in the absence of those preconditions, fulfilled his predictions all too well. Yet if that failure has not by itself proved him wrong, the fact remains that, on the eve of the twenty-first century, socialists do not seem to have very much to be optimistic about.

The Manifesto and the Future

But the story is not finished. Nor have we reached the end of what the *Manifesto* has to teach us. There is still much to be learned even from its predictions. Marx has been proved uncannily right about many things, but nowhere has he been vindicated more completely than in his account of capitalist expansion. It is true that he underestimated the durability of capitalism and how long it could keep on expanding. But for all today's fashionable talk about "globalization," it would be hard to find a more effective description of what is happening today than what he wrote 150 years ago. Capitalism has indeed "battered down all Chinese walls" (including the "walls" of "communist" China), creating a global market and compelling "all nations, on pain of extinction, to adopt the bourgeois mode of production." Capitalism has indeed created a world "after its own image."

In Marx's day, that process of "globalization" was still in its early stages. But today capitalist imperatives of accumulation and competition really do reach into every corner of the world. Many people have argued that this is the final and irreversible triumph of capitalism. Yet in the face of events like the recent financial crisis in Southeast Asia, in economies hailed only yesterday as "Asian tigers," these triumphalist pronouncements have a somewhat hollow ring. Mainstream economists who usually like to use more benign terms like "business cycles," or "slumps," or "recessions" are uttering the word "crisis" with increasing frequency, and some more pessimistic commentators have gone beyond Marxists in their talk of "collapse." Against that background, the *Manifesto*'s portrayal of capitalist expansion as a deeply contradictory process is rather more convincing than capitalist triumphalism:

> a society that has conjured up such gigantic means of production and exchange is like the sorcerer who is no longer able to control the powers of the nether world whom he has called up by his spells.... It is enough to mention the commercial crises that by their periodical return put the existence of the entire bourgeois society on trial.... In these crises, there breaks out an epidemic that, in all earlier epochs, would have seemed an absurdity—the epidemic of over-production....

And, the *Manifesto* continues, the very methods on which capital relies to overcome these crises are the very methods by which it paves the way for more destructive crises and reduces the means of correcting and preventing them.

Capitalism, for instance, used to escape its internal crises by moving outward, into new markets and colonies. Today, having become a virtually universal system, it no longer has the same scope for external expansion which used to save it from its internal contradictions, so it has become subject to those contradictions in historically new ways. Capital today no longer seems able to sustain maximum profitability by means of commensurate economic growth. It is now relying more and more on simply *redistributing* wealth in favor of the rich, and on increasing inequalities, within and between national economies, with the help of the "neoliberal" state. In advanced capitalist countries, the most visible signs of that redistribution are a growing polarization between rich and poor, and the attack on the welfare state. So it is not just in the occasional dramatic crisis but in its "normal" and long-term development that capitalism has been vindicating Marx's predictions about its contradictory expansion.

These developments may after all prove Marx right about the effects of capitalism on the political development of the working class. The conditions that led him to his conclusions about the formation of working class consciousness and organization are still present; and the working class, strategically situated at the heart of capitalism, is still the only social force with the capacity to transform it. At the same time, capitalism is evolving in ways that may overcome the factors that have up to now worked against those processes of class formation.

As neoliberal states step up their attacks on social provision and adopt austerity measures to enhance "flexibility," the complicity between the state and "globalized" capital is becoming increasingly transparent. As a result, it may turn out that economic class struggles will indeed move onto the political plane, and that the working class will indeed be unified in new and unprecedented ways. In many countries, labor movements which have been dormant for some time show signs of reawakening. And we have certainly seen many dramatic examples recently of people joining together in the streets—from Canada to Mexico to France to South Korea—to protest "neoliberalism," "globalization," and all the policies that capitalist states today are implementing to maintain the "competitiveness" of their own national economies.

Contrary to much conventional wisdom today, "globalization" has made the state not less but more important to capital. Capital needs the state to maintain the conditions of accumulation and "competitiveness" in various ways, including direct subsidies at tax-payers' expense; to preserve labor discipline and social order in the face of austerity and "flexibility"; to enhance the mobility of capital while blocking the mobility of labor; to administer huge rescue operations for capitalist economies in crisis (yesterday Mexico, today the "Asian tigers")—operations often organized by international agencies but always paid for by national taxes and enforced by national governments. Even the imperialism of the major capitalist states requires the collaboration of subordinate states to act as transmission belts and agents of enforcement. "Neoliberalism" is not just a withdrawal of the state from social provision. It is a set of active policies, a new form of state intervention designed to enhance capitalist profitability in an integrated global market.

Capital's need for the state makes the state again an important and concentrated focus for class struggle. And the fact that the state is visibly implicated in class exploitation has consequences for class organization and consciousness. It may help to overcome the fragmentation of the working class and create a new unity against a common enemy. It may also help to turn class struggle into political struggle.

Whatever happens, the *Manifesto*'s critique of capitalism and its vision of socialism will remain very much alive as long as capitalism exists. Parts of the *Manifesto*'s political program have been implemented within capitalist society. Child labor in factories has generally been abolished in advanced capitalist countries, though it still exists on a large scale, for instance, in U.S. agriculture, and it is certainly widespread in third world economies—often exploited by "transnationals" based in Western capitalist countries. Progressive income tax is the general rule—though it is under growing attack from the right. In advanced capitalist countries there is free education for all, up to a point—though even this is being eroded now in various ways. Some means of communication and transportation, as well as other enterprises, are, or have been, in public ownership in capitalist societies, and some capitalist countries have state banks.

All this has happened without destroying the capitalist system. In fact, capitalism has been saved from its own destructive tendencies by the public services, the social provision, and the "safety nets" that working class movements in the past have struggled long and hard to achieve.

The kind of public ownership we know today has, to be sure, little in common with enterprises run under direct democratic control, by "free associations of direct producers." For that matter, even public enterprises themselves—not just the means of communication and transportation, but health care and education—can be, and in capitalism are, subjected to the logic of the capitalist market. The objective of today's neoliberal politics is to "privatize" anything that could conceivably be run for capitalist profit—from prisons, to postal services, to old-age pensions. But it has also set out to ensure that every public enterprise, every social service, that cannot be profitably "privatized" will still be subject to market imperatives.

Here, then, is another contradiction: capitalism today, in its efforts to remain "competitive," is destroying the very services and institutions that have often rescued it from self-destruction. But even if neoliberalism does not completely succeed in its wrecking operations, the capitalist system will always restrict any efforts to limit the damage it does to people and nature. It begins to looks as if the logic of the system has now reached the point where the destructive force of capitalism is outstripping its capacity to repair or compensate for the harm it inflicts.

Capitalism will also always restrict the scope of democracy. It can never permit a truly democratic society where there are no oppressed and oppressing classes; where "accumulated labor is but a means to widen, to enrich, to promote the existence of the laborer" and not just to enhance capitalist profit; where reproduction, child care, and relations between the sexes are not deformed by capitalist imperatives; where no nation oppresses another; where culture is free of distortion by the market; and so on. As long as we live under capitalism, we will live in a society where the needs and actions of undemocratic and unaccountable capitalist enterprises, both by the direct exercise of class power and through the "market," shape our social and natural environment and determine the conditions of life for every living being that comes within their global orbit.

Now more than ever it should be obvious, as it was to Marx and Engels, that a society driven by the imperatives of capital accumulation has to give way to a more humane and democratic social order. For such a transformation to take place, the main moving force will still have to be class struggle.